ARISTOS

ARISTOS

Muse Lee

For Norah Borus.

Contents

ABOUT ARISTOS

While sorting through some junk, I dug up a middle school planner that was almost completely blank except for "ACHILLES + PATROCLUS=♥" scrawled majestically in purple marker. My teachers would be disappointed to learn that over a decade later, I'm doing the exact same thing, only in musical form.

Our story begins in summer of 2019. It was a few weeks after college graduation, and I'd reached back into my childhood *Iliad* obsession to create a little Achilles/Patroclus duet. Hoping to get a quick demo before I shipped myself off to grad school, I posted on my Broadway fan account that I was looking for actors to sing my new song. I got an unexpected deluge of inquiries—not from professionals, but from theatre kids and Greek mythology nerds who were just as in love with the story as I once was, all clamoring to be a part of this new gay *Iliad* musical.

The only problem was that it didn't exist. What else could I do but write it?

Thus, *Aristos* found its tentative beginnings in a series of closet demos, a summer of workshop sessions in stuffy practice rooms, and a group of young artists with nothing but a gleam in their eyes and a story to tell. As our show and our community came together, strangers became collaborators, collaborators became friends.

I didn't make it to grad school.

We had just begun to dream of everything *Aristos* could become when the pandemic hit. This might have put a stop to the project, were it not for the fact that we needed it then more than ever. Cheered on by our fast-growing social media fanbase, our unlikely team embarked on the ambitious project of producing a crowd-funded remote album during quarantine. The small California crew grew to an international ensemble, ranging in age from 13 to 70 and representing seven different countries. Scribbles and demos became sheet music and album tracks; readings and livestreams became packed virtual performances and once-in-a-lifetime invitations. And, eventually, it all came together and became 200,000 streams and counting.

Now, with the album wrapped up, I look towards a new phase of this project: adapting *Aristos* for live performance and getting it onstage. A lot is about to change. So, I wanted to finally share the unabridged libretto with you before it becomes whatever it becomes.

From the bottom of my heart, thank you for supporting *Aristos*. I confess that at heart, I'm still that weird tomboy on the playground looking for someone to play gods and heroes with me. Come sit on the swings. I'll tell you a cool story about some of my very oldest friends.

ACHILLES + PATROCLUS=♥,
Muse Lee

DRAMATIS PERSONAE

<u>LEAD</u>

Patroclus

Male, 20s.

Practical, philosophical, and tough, with something dangerous just beneath the surface. An old soul; a young soldier who grew up too fast. Reckons stubbornly with loss before it even happens. Knows himself and the story he is a part of so brutally well. Fights for the Greeks alongside his lifelong companion, Achilles.

Achilles

Male, 20s.

Not quite the golden boy of myth—rather, a soldier running from the choices he made when he was too young to understand them. Intuitive and emotionally perceptive. Carries an innocence that verges on cruelty. Fights for the Greeks alongside his lifelong companion, Patroclus. Largely spoken; must be a very strong actor. Guitar ability preferred.

Odysseus

Male, middle-aged.

A man of many turns. Deftly plays the roles of soldier, advisor, mediator, strategist, and father figure, depending on what will win him advantage. These are always just performances. However, after ten years of war, it is difficult not to become what one has become. Fights for the Greeks. Must be both a compelling speaker and a robust singer.

Briseis

Female, late teens/20s.

A young woman full of quiet cunning. Trojan captive in the Greek camp. Sharp; glistens darkly like a hidden blade. Carries herself with the pride of someone with nothing to lose. If possible, cast a fresh face: someone who audiences have not seen before, someone whose rawness is their power.

SUPPORTING

Young Patroclus

Male, 8-13.

Introverted, sometimes brooding, and alarmingly sharp-witted.

Young Achilles

Male, 8-13.

A tiny force of nature. Emotionally insightful beyond his years. Guitar ability a plus.

Middle Patroclus

Male, mid-to-late teens.

Certain of who he is and what he wants. Acts older than he is, or tries to. Canny enough to see the agenda behind the narratives, but naïve enough to play into them nonetheless.

Middle Achilles

Male, mid-to-late teens.

Cuts to the heart. Speaks plainly and frankly, but there's poetry in it. Learning how to become the man he's expected to be—even as he wavers, poised on the verge of change he isn't ready for.

Thetis

Female, middle-aged.

Mother of Achilles. There is something timeless in her air of long-past tragedy. She is a dream, a story, a memory, and perhaps this makes her a goddess. The voice in Achilles' head urging him to survive the war—at any cost.

Phoenix

Male, 50+.

Second father to Achilles. Universally respected in the Greek camp. Knows no love that isn't touched by grief. The keeper of story and memory.

Ajax

Male, 20s.

Childhood friend of Achilles and Patroclus. Brusque, rash, artless, but there's something tender in the truth that blooms from his rawness.

Priam

Male, 50+.

King of the Trojans. Father of Hector. The rich weave of dignity has worn thin over a decade of grief. This is not a man who has simply lost hope: this is a man who gripped hope with both hands as it was pulled away from him. Mostly spoken; must be a very strong actor.

Pyrrhus

Male, teens.

Coltish, eager son of Achilles, dazzled by ideas of glory and heroism. Carries on what he believes to be his father's legacy. Should remind us painfully of Young Achilles. Almost completely spoken.

Agamemnon

Male, middle-aged.

The brash and egotistical commander of the Greek army. Despite his boorishness, one needs to believe that the sound of his voice could lead armies into battle year after year.

Talthybius

Male, any age.

Herald. Always in a dozen places at once. A wry, charismatic commentator on the goings-on of the Greek camp.

Iphis

Female, any age.

Trojan captive in the Greek camp. Thoughtful, cautious, and spiritual in her own way. An observer, aware of the smallest details.

Diomede

Female, any age.

Trojan captive in the Greek camp. Relentlessly practical and forward-looking. A protector. Cuts right to the truth.

Iphis and Diomede first appear silently in the background of major scenes and move slowly to the forefront over the course of the show. Should be powerful solo and blend well with an ensemble, but do not have to sound like trained musical theatre singers; rather, their voices should instantly tell a story.

ENSEMBLE

Soldiers

Male, all ages.

Soldiers in the Greek army. Should have a smooth, rigorously classical sound. Odysseus, Ajax, Phoenix, and Agamemnon all fall under this category.

Captives

Female, all ages.

Captive women in the Greek camp, ripped away from their homelands. While they should be strong singers, they should also have the quality of real people singing a protest song together. Iphis and Diomede fall under this category.

Dancers

Any genders and ages.

They depict in abstract the most mythic moments of the show: the battles, the funerals, the journeys home, the telling of ancient stories. Note that Chiron and Hector, not included in the cast of characters but mentioned in the script, fall under this category.

The denoted ages are guidelines rather than requirements. Actors of all genders and ethnicities are welcome to audition for any roles.

STAGING NOTES

In its language and its perspective on the source material, *Aristos* mixes the classical and the contemporary. While a terse modern staging would serve the story just as well as a lavish sword-and-sandals production, interpreters of *Aristos* are invited to mix these two modes in a way that is consciously theatrical and representational: think cardboard shields, oil drum amphorae, crowns of twisted wire. Specifically, the all-important lyre is meant to be represented by an acoustic guitar.

Aristos primarily plays out in a war camp. All other scenes occupy the metaphysical realms of story and memory, and do not require a separate set.

ACT I:
PATROCLUS

MOUNT PELION

House dims. The ensemble supplies the call of birds, the breath of the wind, the hum of summer flies. Like figures running around a vase, Young Achilles, Young Patroclus, and Chiron cross the stage in vignette after vignette.

Under Chiron's auspices, the children run, hunt, duel, constellations wheeling through the summer sky. The scenes are unmistakably classical; its heroes are not. What we see are two boys and their old man. It is afternoon. It is afternoon forever.

House goes dark. The overture ends, and the story begins.

A wash of golden light. Young Patroclus is walking along in no great hurry, stepping over rocks and balancing on tree roots.

Like a change in the wind, like a sudden shift of light, Young Achilles appears with his lyre.

[YOUNG ACHILLES] *strumming*
TOMORROW PERHAPS WE'LL GO—

[YOUNG PATROCLUS] *not in the mood*
Not again.

[YOUNG ACHILLES]
I'm not finished. Wait.

TOMORROW PERHAPS WE'LL GO—

He is laughing too hard to finish.

[YOUNG PATROCLUS]
Chiron is waiting for us.

[YOUNG ACHILLES]
Listen.

Young Achilles begins to play. He is just learning this song. It isn't going well.

TOMORROW PERHAPS WE'LL GO RUNNING
OR MAYBE WE'LL WALK BY THE OCEAN
THE TIDE MAKES THE SUMMER-WARM SAND LOSE
ITS MEMORY
OUR FOOTPRINTS WILL FADE WITH THE MORNING

[YOUNG PATROCLUS]
Let's go.

[YOUNG ACHILLES]
TOMORROW PERHAPS WE'LL BE SEABIRDS
TOMORROW PERHAPS CONSTELLATIONS

WE'LL DREAM OF THE GODS'
ENDLESS SUMMER AND THEN
WE WILL WAKE TO THE WAYS
THEY HAVE CHANGED US

He assumes a joking, improvisatory manner, and so does his lyre playing.

AND WHO REALLY KNOWS IF THEY HATE US?
A CURSE OR A BLESSING, IT'S ALL JUST THE SAME
WE'LL TURN INTO TREES LIKE WE'RE LOVERS

Young Patroclus plucks the lyre from his hands.

[YOUNG PATROCLUS]
And if we don't go back now, Chiron will kill us. Come on.

Young Achilles reaches up to take back his lyre, but Young Patroclus steps out of his reach. Young Achilles leaps to his feet to chase him down and wrestle it back. Finally, Young Patroclus is laughing.

The two stumble to the ground under the shade of a fig tree. They catch their breath. Young Achilles idly picks at his lyre. His mood returning, Young Patroclus plucks a fig from the tree and throws it at Young Achilles.

What are you doing here, Achilles?

Young Achilles catches it easily, barely pausing his lyre playing.

[YOUNG ACHILLES]
Chiron sent me to find you.

He lobs the fig back to Young Patroclus.

Do you think the figs are ripe yet?

[YOUNG PATROCLUS]
Not for a little longer.

[YOUNG ACHILLES]
How can you tell?

[YOUNG PATROCLUS]
They're supposed to be purple.

They toss the fig back and forth.

[YOUNG ACHILLES]
Chiron says some figs stay green.

[YOUNG PATROCLUS]
Fine. Try one and poison yourself.

[YOUNG ACHILLES]
I wouldn't be poisoned by an unripened fig.

[YOUNG PATROCLUS]
How would you know? You've never tried it.

Young Patroclus plucks a fig off the tree.

This one looks ripe.

He tosses it to Young Achilles, gently this time, an offering.
The boy bites into it eagerly.

[YOUNG ACHILLES]
You know the other boys don't mean it, Patroclus. They just
like to feel important.

[YOUNG PATROCLUS] *an obvious lie*
It doesn't bother me.

[YOUNG ACHILLES]
Yes, it does.

It isn't right. They shouldn't talk to you like that.

No response except tension in the air.
Young Achilles continues to devour.

I wonder if the gods miss eating figs.
Maybe it gets dull after a while.

He thinks; declares his conclusion while taking another bite.

I would never tire of eating figs.

He offers a bemused Young Patroclus the other half.

[YOUNG PATROCLUS]
Aren't sparring lessons still going?

[YOUNG ACHILLES]
They'll be over by the time we get back.

[YOUNG PATROCLUS]
They're your favorite.

[YOUNG ACHILLES]
You noticed?

[YOUNG PATROCLUS]
It's not too hard to tell. You're really good.

A warm, tentative moment. Then:

The gods drink ambrosia. They don't eat figs.

[YOUNG ACHILLES]
But they'd remember what figs are like.

[YOUNG PATROCLUS]
They never would've tasted figs.

[YOUNG ACHILLES]
The ones who became gods. The ones who were mortals first.

[YOUNG PATROCLUS]
No god is mortal first.

Mortals can't become gods. Those are just the stories they tell
heroes to—

[YOUNG ACHILLES]
To what?

[YOUNG PATROCLUS]
You know.

They turn to face each other.

[YOUNG ACHILLES]
You believe that?

[YOUNG PATROCLUS]
You believe that?

You have grass in your hair.

[YOUNG ACHILLES]
Where?

Young Patroclus uproots a handful of grass and rubs it into Young Achilles' hair. A noise of indignation; a tussle. Young Achilles is glowing.

[YOUNG PATROCLUS] *conciliatory*
Maybe Chiron knows how people get turned into gods.

[YOUNG ACHILLES]
I wouldn't want to become one.

[YOUNG PATROCLUS]
Me neither.

We should go back. If Chiron sent you to find me.

[YOUNG ACHILLES]
I would have come anyway.

Neither makes a move to leave.

What would you become? If the gods could change you into anything.

[YOUNG PATROCLUS] *with satisfaction*
A dog.

[YOUNG ACHILLES]
A dog?

[YOUNG PATROCLUS]
Or a horse. Or a raincloud.

[YOUNG ACHILLES]
Why a raincloud?

[YOUNG PATROCLUS]
I could follow you around and bother you.

What about you, Achilles?

In the orchestra, the melody of "Who Is This Boy?" begins quietly.

If the gods could change you, what would you become?

[YOUNG ACHILLES]
I don't know.

[YOUNG PATROCLUS]
Just pick something.

[YOUNG ACHILLES]
Anything.

[YOUNG PATROCLUS]
Anything?

[YOUNG ACHILLES]
Anything. I'd become whatever you are.

It was a joke, at least before he said it.

[YOUNG PATROCLUS]
Then we shouldn't change at all.

It is both a secret and the simplest thing in the world.

The orchestra swells with the Memory Theme as the ensemble rushes in, leaves on the wind as seasons pass and return. A war camp is assembled; a world is deconstructed and pieced back together. Yet, the boys remain, and Young Achilles plays his lyre:

[YOUNG ACHILLES]
WE'LL DREAM OF THE GODS'
ENDLESS SUMMER AND THEN
WE WILL WAKE TO THE WAYS

THEY HAVE CHANGED US

TOMORROW PERHAPS I
WILL SLEEP PAST THE SUNRISE
AND FIND THAT YOU'VE GONE IN THE NIGHT
TIE WINGS TO MY SANDALS
I'LL DRINK FROM THE SKY
AND I'LL BE BY YOUR SIDE BY AND BY

'CAUSE WHERE YOU GO
I WILL GO WITH
I WILL GO WITH YOU

OH, DON'T YOU KNOW
MY CHILDHOOD IN IS YOUR EYES
BRIGHT AND WISE

WE'LL TAKE OUR TIME
DON'T LEAVE ME BEHIND
I WILL GO WITH YOU
I WILL GO WITH YOU
I WILL GO WITH YOU

WHERE YOU GO

II

THE EMBASSY

The war camp is fully assembled. Against firepits and military tents, Young Achilles and Young Patroclus do not notice their utter displacement.

[YOUNG ACHILLES]

Race you back to Chiron.

[YOUNG PATROCLUS]

No, you won't.

[YOUNG ACHILLES]

Bet you I'll get there first.

[YOUNG PATROCLUS]

No, you won't.

[YOUNG ACHILLES]

Bet you the last of my pork roast.

Enter Middle Patroclus and Middle Achilles.

[MIDDLE PATROCLUS]
You're going to let me win.

[MIDDLE ACHILLES]
No, I won't.

[MIDDLE PATROCLUS]
Yes, you will.

[MIDDLE ACHILLES]
No, I won't.

[MIDDLE PATROCLUS]
Prove it.

Middle Patroclus snatches the lyre from Young Achilles' hands. All run off as Achilles and Patroclus enter. Achilles settles on a stool with his lyre, and Patroclus stands beside him.

To sparse acoustic accompaniment, with Young Achilles singing with him from offstage:

[ACHILLES]
'CAUSE WHERE YOU GO
I WILL GO WITH

[ACHILLES & YOUNG ACHILLES]
I WILL GO WITH YOU

[ACHILLES]
OH, DON'T YOU KNOW

[ACHILLES & YOUNG ACHILLES]
MY CHILDHOOD IN IS YOUR EYES

[YOUNG ACHILLES]
BRIGHT AND WISE

The music grows mellower, the accompaniment more sparse, as Patroclus assumes the melody in a soft, conversational tone.

[PATROCLUS]
YOU MEET MY EYES
YOU SOFTLY REPLY…

As Achilles reaches the end of his song, Ajax, Odysseus, and Phoenix enter. They do not yet venture into Achilles' tent. Instead, they stop a little away from the entrance; Odysseus is giving final instructions to the group. Patroclus and Achilles are unaware of their presence.

To gentle accompaniment, Achilles sings.

[ACHILLES]
I WILL GO WITH YOU

And again, for reassurance.

I WILL GO WITH YOU

[ACHILLES & PATROCLUS]
I WILL GO WITH YOU…

A tentative moment between them. Then, Patroclus notices the men. A subtle gesture to get Achilles' attention.

[ODYSSEUS]
A lovely tune. Pity that we only caught the end of it.

[ACHILLES]
Welcome, friends.

[PATROCLUS]
Odysseus. Ajax. Phoenix.

An exchanged glance with Achilles. A nonverbal conversation.

The meal is almost ready, if you'd like to join us for dinner.

[ODYSSEUS]
We would never object to that, would we?

The men come inside the tent. Odysseus shrugs off his purple cloak and leaves it on a chair. In the background, captive women Iphis and Diomede slip in quietly to set the table, then just as quietly retreat. Patroclus turns to finish preparations, and Achilles follows after.

[PATROCLUS]
Something must have happened. Agamemnon is finally begging you to fight.

[ACHILLES]
He could have come himself.

[PATROCLUS]
He's desperate. He sent all his cleverest men.

[ACHILLES]
And Ajax.

Patroclus reprimands him, but cannot help his laughter.

Odysseus speaks, and the pair turns around.

[ODYSSEUS]
TWELVE STALLIONS

[PHOENIX]
SEVEN TRIPODS

[AJAX]
AND TEN BARS OF GOLD

[PHOENIX]
TWENTY CAULDRONS

[AJAX]
SEVEN WOMEN

[ODYSSEUS]
AND PLUNDERED GOODS GALORE

[ODYSSEUS, AJAX, & PHOENIX]
A DOWRY, A DAUGHTER
A MARRIAGE AND A TREASURE

CHRYSOTHEMIS, LAODICE, OR IPHIANASSA

Lights, suddenly, on the rest of the camp: the soldiers idling at their posts, the captives airing out the laundry, all spreading the word of Agamemnon's outrageous offer.

[ODYSSEUS, AJAX, PHOENIX, & ENSEMBLE]
CARDAMYLE AND ENOPE
THE GRASSY HILLS OF HIRE,
AND PHERAE THE SACROSANCT
ANTHEA DEEP IN MEADOWS—

[ODYSSEUS]
BRISEIS

[PHOENIX]
BRISEIS

[AJAX]
BRISEIS

[ODYSSEUS] *with finality*
Briseis.

Focus snaps back to the small group gathered in Achilles' tent. At the mention of Briseis' name, Iphis and Diomede exchange a glance and retreat to refill the wine jug, listening in all the while.

[ACHILLES]
These names mean nothing to me.

[ODYSSEUS]

Agamemnon swears that Briseis has not been harmed. He is more than willing to return your slave girl, and restore your honor—

[AJAX]

Not to mention the gifts, and the cities, and the women—

[ODYSSEUS]

—if you, and your Myrmidons, fight with us against Hector.

[ACHILLES]

None of you fought for me when Agamemnon dishonored me.

[ODYSSEUS]

Then who will remember you if you don't fight for him?

[ACHILLES]

I won't be remembered for this humiliation. We've been fighting at Troy for ten years now. And all for what? For some king's runaway wife? Is he the only man alive who loves somebody, Odysseus?

Achilles has hit a nerve.

[ODYSSEUS]

INDULGE ME, ACHILLES. EXPLAIN WHY THIS IS SO— WE CAN'T ALL BE HEROES, BUT SADLY, SO IT GOES— YOU BARGAIN FOR GLORY, BUT WILL NOT PAY THE PRICE

THE MEN FIND IT FUNNY, AND FRANKLY SO DO I

Odysseus resumes his casual, conversational air.

Tomorrow, Hector's army will breach our camp and burn our ships. Tomorrow, our dream of return will come to ash. We will never be able to go home, Achilles. The story nears its ending, and it's time for you to assume your place in it.

If not for your own life, for your legacy. Isn't that what you came to Troy to ensure?

A beat.

[ACHILLES]
I don't want to waste your evening, friends.

If you want to save yourselves, sail home. I won't go to war for Agamemnon. Not until he comes to beg at my feet and apologize for taking Briseis.

Stunned silence. Then:

[AJAX]
You can't do this to us.

[ODYSSEUS]
Leave it.

[AJAX]
He can't do this to us.

Do you think we want to be here any more than / you do?

[PHOENIX]
/ Ajax, please.

[AJAX]
Just because we aren't great enough for prophecies doesn't mean we won't be feasts for crows. It may be news to you, but no one wants to die here.

[ACHILLES]
It's late. We should say goodnight.

[PHOENIX]
Achilles. My prince. Wait.

In the orchestra, Phoenix's Theme begins.

You all know of my misfortune. The gods decreed that I would never bear children of my own, but that didn't matter once your father took me in. You were just a baby. Of course, you spat up on me and fussed in my arms, but you refused to go to the royal banquets with anyone else. Nobody else was allowed to cut your meat or hold your cup. Only old Phoenix.

I can't blame you for your anger. None of us can. But indulge me. I only wish for you to hear this one story. Of course, you know of the great hero Meleager. But have you heard the story of his beloved?

[PATROCLUS]
Who?

Phoenix looks directly at him.

[PHOENIX]
Cleopatra.

An actor ushers in the tent's fourth wall, and we watch Phoenix narrating the story in silhouette to his gathered audience. Dancers representing Cleopatra and Meleager flicker through, their shadows looming large.

III

PHOENIX

*T*he wall ripples back to reveal Achilles and Patroclus' tent, now just
about empty. In a corner, Patroclus is spreading a bedroll for
Phoenix to sleep on.

[PATROCLUS]

We can keep a bed for you here.

[PHOENIX]

Oh, don't bother.

[PATROCLUS]

That way, Achilles and I won't have to go back and forth every
day. It'll save us all some trouble.

[PHOENIX]

You know me better than that. I just need to catch my breath.
You'll find me scaling the cliffs tomorrow morning.

[PATROCLUS]

Not even Achilles can scale those cliffs, Phoenix.

[PHOENIX]
I wouldn't put it past him. Remember the oak tree on the hill behind the running path? It was before you came to the house. I guess you wouldn't have been there.

[PATROCLUS] *with humor and indulgence*
I think I've heard the story before.

[PHOENIX]
By sunset, there was a whole crowd gathered at the bottom, begging him to stop climbing. Turns out he just didn't know how to get down.

Both laugh.

[PATROCLUS]
If anyone could have convinced him, it would have been the three of you.

[PHOENIX]
I knew all those gifts wouldn't make a difference. Odysseus saw it clearly. Achilles' rage, his refusal to fight...of course it isn't about his commander taking his slave, not really.

[PATROCLUS]
No. It's not about Briseis.

[PHOENIX]
Lovely girl. But I've fought in many wars, Patroclus. Every soldier has his dark night of the soul. You follow a man to the ends of the earth, and at last, you come to hate the very sight of him.

He could give you his kingdom and the clothes off his back, but it will never match up to what you gave him.

It isn't an uncommon story. It's only that most men can't do much about it.

[PATROCLUS]

Most men aren't Achilles.

[PHOENIX]

You can say that again.

[PATROCLUS]

I liked the story you told us tonight. Chiron told us about Meleager when we were boys.

[PHOENIX]

Did he?

[PATROCLUS]

Mm. He was Meleager's teacher.

[PHOENIX]

No surprise. The great horseman trained every Greek soldier worth something. You and Achilles and Ajax and everyone who came before you.

[PATROCLUS]

He never mentioned a lover named Cleopatra.

Phoenix hears his unspoken question and dismisses it.

[PHOENIX]
Too unpleasant for a bedtime story.

[PATROCLUS] *letting it go*
We weren't paying too much attention, anyway.

[PHOENIX]
You know I never could have children myself. Chiron was blessed to gain so many.

[PATROCLUS]
But all heroes. I don't know how he survived it.

[PHOENIX]
I feel for the old king of Troy, you know. He's enduring the same. At least his Hector still survives. And as long as Hector lives, so too will Achilles.

[PATROCLUS]
At least we have that assurance.

[PHOENIX]
I suppose prophecies are good for something.

[PATROCLUS]
It does ease my mind. No one besides Achilles stands a chance against Hector. And Achilles won't fight him.

[PHOENIX]
It seems to me that the solution is simple. We just shouldn't be at war with each other.

Patroclus finishes making Phoenix's bed.

[PATROCLUS]
There we go. You'll be alright?

[PHOENIX]
Of course I will.

[PATROCLUS]
Only making sure.

Patroclus begins to exit.

[PHOENIX]
Patroclus? Before it's too late.

Patroclus exits and is alone. He stands outside the tent, deep in thought. Then, he notices Achilles down the beach, sitting at the edge of the water, talking to someone in a pocket of illumination. Thetis is holding counsel with her son.

IV

ARISTOS ACHAION

After checking on Phoenix one last time, Patroclus goes to Achilles slowly, but keeps his distance. As he approaches, the ensemble supplies the soft sound of ocean waves.

[THETIS]
ACHILLEUS, WILL YOU NOT HEED?
THERE IS NEWS THAT I BRING FROM OLYMPUS
THE GODS HAVE BEEN TOLD OF A PROPHECY
OF WHICH I HAVE COME TO APPRISE YOU

WILL YOU NOT HEED?
WILL YOU NOT HEED?
WILL YOU NOT HEED?

ARISTOS
ARISTOS ACHAION
MY SORROW

[ACHILLES]
Mother.

[THETIS]

Tomorrow, Hector will breach the camp and burn the ships.

[ACHILLES]

You're sure.

[THETIS]

Everyone knows the Greeks cannot win without you. If you don't fight for them, Zeus will continue to shower glory on the Trojans. That is not what I've come to tell you.

[ACHILLES]

Then?

[THETIS]

Tomorrow, the Best of the Myrmidons will fall at Trojan hands.

[ACHILLES]

Hector isn't dead. I haven't–

[THETIS]

I know. So hold back from fighting Hector and you'll be safe, Achilles. We know what the seers say. As long as Hector lives, you will live. It won't be you.

[ACHILLES]

Who is the Best of the Myrmidons, then?

[THETIS]

Don't think about it. That's not for us to know.

You are safe. It's good news.

She touches his braided lock of hair.

It's growing so long.

[ACHILLES]
It's completely out of hand.

[THETIS]
Come here.

She unfastens it from its place, loosens it, and begins to rebraid it.

[ACHILLES]
I look silly.

[THETIS]
You have to keep this braid, Achilles. Remember what you
promised me.

[ACHILLES]
I'll only cut it when I return home safe. I know.

He flinches away from his mother's ministrations.

Ow.

[THETIS]
You did well in refusing King Agamemnon's embassy today.
Our plan is working.

[ACHILLES]

The Greeks are dying without me.

[THETIS]

The Greeks are dying because of Agamemnon. He is a stubborn, foolish man. He took your slave Briseis, who you righteously won in battle. He humiliated you in front of everybody. All for his own dog-faced greed. If he refuses to follow the customs of his own army and grant a loyal soldier his dues, what right does he have to ask that you give your life for him?

[ACHILLES]

No right at all.

[THETIS]

And if you win this war for him, who will enjoy the wealth and the glory?

[ACHILLES]

He will.

[THETIS]

Without you and your Myrmidons, his entire army will be killed. You make him desperate for you.

[ACHILLES]

I thought Agamemnon would've relented a long time ago.
I didn't mean it to go this far.

[THETIS]

Agamemnon's a fool, but he's still a leader of men.

If he allows this massacre, his soldiers will mutiny. He knows this. Tomorrow. Tomorrow, the Trojans will storm the camp and he'll see the cost of his stubbornness.

[ACHILLES]

He'll beg at my feet for forgiveness.

[THETIS]

And he'll give you back your honor.

[ACHILLES]

And then?

[THETIS]

Then what?

[ACHILLES]

Then, will I fight?

[THETIS]

No need to think about tomorrow. Today, you're still alive.

Be safe tomorrow, Achilles. The gods watch over you.

ARISTOS

ARISTOS ACHAION...

She vanishes, and the surreal cast of light dissolves with her. Achilles and Patroclus are alone for the first time that evening.

[ACHILLES]

Patroclus.

[PATROCLUS]

Hey.

[ACHILLES]

Come feel the water. The ocean's warm tonight.

[PATROCLUS]

What are you up to this time?

[ACHILLES]

It *is.* The afternoons are getting longer and longer. Maybe in a few days, we'll have enough light left to go—

As Achilles is speaking, Patroclus goes over unthinkingly, entirely forgetting his suspicion. Achilles immediately splashes him.

[PATROCLUS]

Rascal.

[ACHILLES]

Wet fool.

A familiar gesture: a flick or a nudge or something entirely their own.

How long have you been standing there?

[PATROCLUS]

You were just staring at the water. I didn't want to interrupt.

[ACHILLES]

Come sit with me.

[PATROCLUS]

Some days, the ocean scares me half to death.

[ACHILLES]

Why?

[PATROCLUS]

I think I've gotten used to it all, but then the moon rises in early summer and everything looks alien.

[ACHILLES]

I think I can see what you mean. You look like—

[PATROCLUS]

Don't finish that sentence.

[ACHILLES]

I was going to say a stag of Artemis. It was a compliment.

[PATROCLUS]

I'm going back. Enjoy your warm water.

He kicks lightly at the water, splashing Achilles in belated reprisal. Then, he begins to cross back to the tent. Achilles follows. They look inside.

[ACHILLES]
Is Phoenix sleeping?

[PATROCLUS]
Pretending to be.

[ACHILLES]
It's a little quiet.

[PATROCLUS]
See, he's…

[ACHILLES]
…that's a blanket.

[PATROCLUS]
No, it's—

That's a blanket.

[ACHILLES]
I'll go find him.

[PATROCLUS]
I *told* him to just stay here tonight.

Achilles begins to exit.

[ACHILLES] *theatric*
He's halfway to Mount Ida by now.

[PATROCLUS]

I'm sure he's fine.

[ACHILLES]

I'll at least make sure he made it to his tent.

[PATROCLUS]

I think he needs time to himself. You know how he is.

[ACHILLES]

I can't blame him. I've had enough company for tonight.

[PATROCLUS]

Good. We're not especially popular in the camp right now.

Patroclus nudges past him into the tent and busies himself with straightening up the table from dinner. Achilles goes to his side to assist.

Did the strays come by yet?

[ACHILLES]

I didn't hear them.

Patroclus collects some scraps in small bowls.

[PATROCLUS]

We were so busy with our dinner that we missed theirs.

Patroclus reaches for another plate. Achilles touches his arm to stop him.

[ACHILLES]
Leave the roast.

[PATROCLUS]
They're hungry.

[ACHILLES]
So are we. Save the pork roast. They'll be all right.

Achilles helps Patroclus set the bowls outside, watching him all the while.

Where are you going?

[PATROCLUS]
What?

[ACHILLES]
You gave them their morning helping, too.

He has been caught.

[PATROCLUS]
I'm wide awake. I think I'll go into the camp.

[ACHILLES]
Now?

[PATROCLUS]
I might go talk to the men, see what's on their minds.

[ACHILLES]
How long will you be gone?

[PATROCLUS]
Depends who I wind up talking to.

A beat. Then, from Patroclus, almost casual:

You haven't changed your mind, have you?

[ACHILLES]
Why would I?

[PATROCLUS]
Then what will you do if they're all—if the worst happens to-morrow?

[ACHILLES]
There's nothing for me to do, Patroclus. It's all up to Agamem-non.

[PATROCLUS]
They're all going to be…

One of you has to budge.

[ACHILLES]
And it won't be me.

[PATROCLUS]
The men say you're unreasonable. Unreasonable and selfish.

[ACHILLES]
And what about you, Patroclus? Do you think so, too?

I'm not condemning anyone to die, Patroclus. Whenever they want, they can lay down their weapons and sail home.

[PATROCLUS]
The men swore to fight for Agamemnon, just like you did.

[ACHILLES]
I swore to fight for a king who'd treat me fairly if I risked my life for him every day. If he won't honor his end of the bargain, the deal is off.

[PATROCLUS]
This is war, Achilles. No one said it was going to be fair.

[ACHILLES]
You enlisted too, Patroclus. Why?

[PATROCLUS]
How long can we put this off, Achilles?

[ACHILLES]
Put what off?

[PATROCLUS]
You know what.

[ACHILLES]
So do you. Say it.

What will happen to me if I give in? Say it, Patroclus.

Patroclus turns away. He pushes aside the tent flaps. As he does, Young Achilles and Young Patroclus run past the tent, singing messy snatches of "Where You Go."

The memory has stricken Patroclus still, and he stands waveringly at the threshold. Achilles waits.

[PATROCLUS]
I should get going.

Achilles nods. Patroclus begins to leave. Achilles' voice reaches out to him across the darkness of the tent.

[ACHILLES]
I left the pork roast for you. You can have it when you get hungry. I saved you the last of mine.

A beat.

[PATROCLUS]
Oh. Come here.

Achilles does. Patroclus adjusts his braid.

If you're going to keep that, at least don't have it sticking out like that.

[ACHILLES]
Bastard.

[PATROCLUS]
Just an exile, actu—

Achilles smacks him before he can finish.

I'll see you when I get back.

[ACHILLES]
All right.

Patroclus leaves—and immediately comes back in, rummaging through their tent.

[PATROCLUS]
Forgot something.

[ACHILLES]
What are you looking for?

He doesn't answer, but he does find it: Odysseus' purple cloak, left behind from that evening.

Is that—?

V

AGAMEMNON

*P*atroclus *waits outside Agamemnon's tent, lost in thought. He reaches out to touch the gleaming helmet resting on a stand.*

Within, Agamemnon is reaching the height of some spectacular tirade, with his herald Talthybius as unfortunate audience.

[AGAMEMNON] *muffled, from within*
And what good is that? What good is any of that?

[TALTHYBIUS] *muffled, from within*
Yes, sir.

[AGAMEMNON] *muffled, from within*
I'll go talk to my brother.

[TALTHYBIUS] *muffled, from within*
Yes, sir.

[AGAMEMNON] *emerging*
He and his precious harlot got us into this situation,

maybe he can get us out. Sounds familiar, doesn't it?

Agamemnon sweeps out through the tent threshold, followed by Talthybius, rousing Patroclus from his reverie. Patroclus snaps to attention.

[PATROCLUS]

King Agamemnon. Good evening, sir.

[AGAMEMNON]

What do you want?

[PATROCLUS]

I wished to convey our gratitude for the gifts you offered us. You have our sincere thanks, sir.

[AGAMEMNON]

Oh, you're welcome. I'm looking forward to shielding the ships from arrows, spears, and the lightning of Zeus with "sincere thanks." Sir.

Agamemnon begins to exit. Patroclus stops him.

[PATROCLUS]

Not all hope is lost.

[AGAMEMNON]

Spoken like a man who won't die in battle tomorrow.

[PATROCLUS]

Sir, you know how Achilles loves Briseis.

He wouldn't have quit the war over her otherwise. I was hoping to speak with her. Bring back some winning words to stir Achilles' heart.

[AGAMEMNON]

I could do that myself.

[PATROCLUS]

With all due respect, sir, do you think that Achilles will listen to you?

[AGAMEMNON]

If I had more hours in the day and fewer thoughts of impending doom, I'd have you strung up for insubordination.

[PATROCLUS]

Yes, sir. I'm sorry, sir.

[AGAMEMNON]

Scram.

Agamemnon exits. Once Agamemnon is out of earshot, Talthybius says:

[TALTHYBIUS]

He usually at least has a sense of humor.

[PATROCLUS]

Not one I enjoy.

[TALTHYBIUS]

Well, me neither. But this is sure to go down as Agamemnon's darkest mood in history.

[PATROCLUS]

That's assuming it doesn't get worse.

Talthybius settles and plays idly with a set of dice, clearly expecting his friend to settle with him, but Patroclus remains standing tense, as if he were still before a superior officer.

[TALTHYBIUS]

That was a good one, though. It was worth a try.

[PATROCLUS]

I didn't think that would work on him. I just wanted to make sure she's all right.

[TALTHYBIUS]

I figured. She's asked about you. In her sly way, of course.

[PATROCLUS]

She hasn't been harmed?

[TALTHYBIUS]

No. Agamemnon wouldn't dare. I heard the embassy was a bust?

[PATROCLUS]

You could say that.

[TALTHYBIUS]

I was afraid it would be. Well, no one's getting much sleep tonight, then. Fancy a round of dice, Patroclus?

[PATROCLUS]

I actually came into camp to look for Odysseus. I wanted to talk to him.

[TALTHYBIUS]

You hate that man.

[PATROCLUS]

He has his moments.

[TALTHYBIUS]

He shouldn't.

If it's any consolation, you two aren't his favorite, either. He would've given anything to have the choice Achilles did. And who can blame him? He doesn't want to be here any more than you do.

He sees Patroclus' reaction, does not push.

I heard he was out spying and raiding along the border. The old fox should be back in his burrow by now.

[PATROCLUS]

Thank you. I'll go by his tent.

[TALTHYBIUS]

Sure you can't spare a dead man a round of dice?

[PATROCLUS]

I owe you one.

[TALTHYBIUS]

Plans for the future. I like that. Go, find Odysseus.

[PATROCLUS]

I will. Thank you. And good luck tomorrow.

[TALTHYBIUS]

We'll all need it.

VI

KLEOS

*O**dysseus is standing by his own tent, hanging his stolen saddles. Patroclus lingers for a moment before addressing him.*

[PATROCLUS]
Would you like a hand with that, Odysseus?

Odysseus' back is turned, but he is unsurprised by Patroclus' voice.

[ODYSSEUS]
Patroclus. Still awake?

[PATROCLUS]
I could ask you the same.

*Patroclus wordlessly goes to help him. The two finish hanging the
saddles, then Odysseus leads Patroclus into the tent as he says:*

[ODYSSEUS]
I don't imagine that sleep is coming easy to anyone tonight.
Wine?

[PATROCLUS]
No, thank you.

Odysseus pours himself a cup while Patroclus hangs back.

[ODYSSEUS]
My son kept the oddest hours in his first few years. His mother and I would be awake all night, waiting for him to demand his rights. I never really adjusted back. Even here, right when I'm about to fall asleep, I'm always half expecting to hear a baby crying.

[PATROCLUS]
I can imagine.

[ODYSSEUS]
Well, I assume you didn't come to hear an old man prattle about his son.

[PATROCLUS]
Before the war began, Achilles took shelter on Skyros. The king owed his mother a favor. He would've been safe there. He knew you'd found out about the prophecy and he said he didn't want to fight. But you arrived on the island, and he changed his mind and enlisted.

[ODYSSEUS]
If you recall, he came entirely on his own accord.

[PATROCLUS]

You went after him. You tempted him with all these
promises—

[ODYSSEUS]

He knew the stakes. He made his choice.

[PATROCLUS]

He had no idea what he was choosing.

[ODYSSEUS]

Of course he did. Boys like him enable wars. Men like him
start them. If not for the Achilleses of Greece, I doubt we'd be
here in the first place.

[PATROCLUS]

We were just boys.

[ODYSSEUS]

And you could have continued as you were. But he wanted to
be Aristos Achaion. Best of the Greeks. He knew the price of his
fame as well as I did.

[PATROCLUS]

Would you have done the same if it were your son?

[ODYSSEUS]

It was not my son. And you and I both know that if Achilles
does not fight for us, I will never see my son again. Forgive me
for attempting to prevent that possibility.

He regains his equanimity.

I know that you both resent me, and not unfairly so. What have you really come to say, Patroclus?

Patroclus is silent for a moment.

[PATROCLUS]
How did you do it?

[ODYSSEUS]
What?

[PATROCLUS]
Convince him to fight. I don't understand.

[ODYSSEUS]
He was a boy hungry for fame. This promised to be the greatest war of the generation. It was a simple thing.

[PATROCLUS]
Not so simple. He'd told his father he wouldn't go.

[ODYSSEUS]
So he turned against his parents. That's how most aspiring heroes get their start.

[PATROCLUS]
Odysseus. He could have had a long, peaceful reign surrounded by his loved ones, or he could die a soldier in a daze of youth and glory. His mother knew before he was even born. The

seers all said that if he fought for you, he'd be killed before the city fell. He knew. And for some reason, he chose this, and he went with you.

Just tell me this. Is there no way you can change his mind again?

A moment.

[ODYSSEUS]
You want that?

[PATROCLUS]
What choice do I have?

[ODYSSEUS]
You know what this would mean for him.

[PATROCLUS]
And so does he. He has always known.

[ODYSSEUS]
Patroclus. I tried my best tonight. We all did. But I convinced him to fight once, and we all know how that turned out for him. There's no chance he will listen to me again.

An idea forms in Odysseus' head. He regards Patroclus carefully.

You know, it is not unlike Phoenix's story. The story of Meleager and Cleopatra. If there's anyone he will heed now, it's not me.

[PATROCLUS]

I actually came to return your cloak. You left it this evening.

He produces the garment.

[ODYSSEUS]

Many thanks. I was wondering where it had gone. Must have been out of my head to leave it lying around like that.

[PATROCLUS]

The embroidery is lovely.

[ODYSSEUS]

A gift from my wife. From our wedding day.

It's very late. I will try to get some rest.

[PATROCLUS]

You won't.

[ODYSSEUS]

I won't. You return to Achilles. Send him my regards.

You won't.

Patroclus gives him a half-smile.

[PATROCLUS]

I won't.

Patroclus lingers a moment longer, then nods farewell to Odysseus. As he quietly leaves, we see Odysseus sitting alone, running his fingers along the borders of the cloak.

VII

CLEOPATRA

*L*eaving the tent behind, Patroclus walks along the sea back to his *own tent. The camp is quiet and empty, and he tilts his head to gaze up at the stars..*

[PATROCLUS]
THEY CAN SEND A THOUSAND EMBASSIES
THEY CAN SLAUGHTER, THEY CAN PRAY
THERE IS NOTHING THAT WILL CRACK HIM
THERE IS NOTHING I CAN SAY

Dancers onstage represent the events that he narrates, their shadows looming large on the tent wall.

OLD PHOENIX SPEAKS OF MELEAGER
A PROUD AND FRAGILE NAME
A HERO WHO WAS WRACKED WITH ANGER
AS HIS CITY WAS AFLAME

THEY BEGGED THE MAN TO FIGHT FOR THEM
HE REFUSED THEM ALL THE SAME

BUT HIS LOVER WATCHED THEIR SUFFERING
AND SHE COULDN'T BEAR THE PAIN

PHOENIX SAYS HER NAME
AND HE LOOKS AT ME
AND WE ALL KNOW WHAT HE MEANS BY THAT

HER PARENTS CALLED HER HALCYON
THE GIRL WHO THEY NAMED CLEOPATRA

CLEOPATRA
SHE WAS ON HER KNEES
IN HER BRILLIANT GRIEF

CLEOPATRA
AND HER EYES WERE DARK
LIKE A PROPHET'S DREAM
CLEOPATRA

SO SHE WENT TO HIM
IN THE FATEFUL DARK
AS THE ASHES FELL LIKE STARS

AND HER TEARS WERE BIRDS
AND THEY TRAVELED FAR
AND THEY NESTED IN HIS HEART

AND HE SAYS HER NAME
AND IT FALLS LIKE SAND
EVERY LETTER COARSE AND FINE

WHEN YOU REARRANGE
THE SYLLABLES
THE NAME SHE BEARS IS MINE

[PATROCLUS & ENSEMBLE]
CLEOPATRA

[PATROCLUS]
THIS HE SWORE TO YOU:
"WHEN THE WAR IS THROUGH

[PATROCLUS & ENSEMBLE]
CLEOPATRA

[PATROCLUS]
WHEN THE WORLD IS NEW
I'LL BE THERE WITH YOU
CLEOPATRA"

HE LOVED HER MORE THAN ANYTHING
HE WENT, HE FOUGHT, HE WON

But it was too late. *She* was too late.

THE DAMAGE HAD BEEN DONE

No honor waited for Meleager. His hands empty, the torch of his fame diminished--he saved his city from disaster, but earned only hatred and disgrace.

Deep in thought, Patroclus ventures to his tent and pushes aside the flap to peek inside. The lights reveal Achilles, fast asleep. Patroclus takes a moment to gaze at him.

AND SHE WENT TO HIM
IN THE FATEFUL DARK
AS THE ASHES FELL LIKE STARS

Patroclus has made his decision. Abruptly, he turns back and walks to Odysseus' tent. Odysseus admits him, and the two are seen in silhouette, talking.

VIII

INTERLUDE I

To signify the beginning of the flashback, Young Achilles and Young Patroclus run across the stage, passing in front of the tent, singing messy snatches of "Where You Go." They exit.

The tent fades out of view. Lights brighten to shimmering evening. Middle Achilles and Middle Patroclus enter, dueling with wooden swords.

[MIDDLE ACHILLES]
Incoming.

Careful. Watch your back.

Whoa. Don't fall for that again.

[MIDDLE PATROCLUS]
Are you supposed to be helping me win?

[MIDDLE ACHILLES]
I'm not. I'm talking through the moves.

Middle Patroclus reaches out and grabs Middle Achilles' sword by its wooden "blade." He tosses it to the side.

[MIDDLE PATROCLUS]
What do you call that one?

[MIDDLE ACHILLES]
Cheating.

With his free hand, Middle Patroclus throws a playful strike; Middle Achilles retaliates. The two fall into a tussle, wooden swords forgotten.

[MIDDLE PATROCLUS]
I surrender! I surrender!

What will you do with yourself next summer? You won't have a dueling partner to boss around. Even Ajax is going.

[MIDDLE ACHILLES]
Well, if my father has any say—

Middle Patroclus raises his eyebrows at him.

We'll be talking it over next time I'm home. He wants me to leave Mount Pelion and start preparing for kingship.

[MIDDLE PATROCLUS]
And?

[MIDDLE ACHILLES]
And what?

[MIDDLE PATROCLUS]

He's been singing that tune all year. What else is new?

[MIDDLE ACHILLES]

He also thinks it's time for me to choose a wife.

Middle Patroclus bursts out laughing.

[MIDDLE PATROCLUS]

Who?

[MIDDLE ACHILLES]

I don't know.

Another round?

Patroclus lies back.

[MIDDLE PATROCLUS]

I'm exhausted.

[MIDDLE ACHILLES]

We've barely even started.

[MIDDLE PATROCLUS]

I'm sleeping.

Middle Achilles pokes him with the sword until he giggles, unable to keep up the pretense any longer.

I was sleeping!

[MIDDLE ACHILLES]

If we wait any longer, the sun will go down.

[MIDDLE PATROCLUS]

You're acting like you've enlisted.

Continued poking.

[MIDDLE ACHILLES]

You're acting like you haven't. You're a warrior now, Patroclus. Up you go.

[MIDDLE PATROCLUS]

I'm beginning to regret that decision.

He is already taking up his wooden sword. As they duel:

[MIDDLE ACHILLES]

It's not too late.

[MIDDLE PATROCLUS]

No?

A surprise attack.

[MIDDLE ACHILLES]

Not too late for me to gain the upper hand.

Middle Patroclus blocks his strike just in time and goes in for the killing blow.

[MIDDLE PATROCLUS]
How about now?

They collapse to the ground and catch their breath.

Keep that up and they'll try to recruit you.

[MIDDLE ACHILLES]
I'll never go. It's a big fuss over nothing.

[MIDDLE PATROCLUS]
Not to them. They'll want swift-footed Achilles on their side.
You've got a reputation.

[MIDDLE ACHILLES]
A reputation.

[MIDDLE PATROCLUS]
You do.

[MIDDLE ACHILLES]
That's probably why my father wants me to come home.

[MIDDLE PATROCLUS] *incredulous*
Because he's worried?

[MIDDLE ACHILLES]
Probably.

[MIDDLE PATROCLUS] *incredulous*
That you'll go?

[MIDDLE ACHILLES]
I mean—

[MIDDLE PATROCLUS]
He's the one who's been preparing you all your life. He sent
you to train here.

[MIDDLE ACHILLES]
But you know what the seers are telling him.

[MIDDLE PATROCLUS]
Do you think it's really true?

[MIDDLE ACHILLES]
I'm not going to find out.

I still don't know why they'd want me. I've never even fought
in a real battle.

[MIDDLE PATROCLUS]
Me neither.

They settle into silence.

[MIDDLE ACHILLES]
I just don't know why they think I'd want to go.

Why anyone would want to go.

Patroclus does not take the bait. Achilles imitates Chiron.

"Dangerous behavior."

[MIDDLE PATROCLUS]
"Dangerous."

[MIDDLE ACHILLES]
"Unwise and unnecessary."

[MIDDLE PATROCLUS]
Unsound and unnecessary.

[MIDDLE ACHILLES]
Unsound and unnecessary. That was what he said.

Patroclus, this might sound silly.

[MIDDLE PATROCLUS]
I'm used to it.

[MIDDLE ACHILLES]
Did you enlist because of Chiron?

[MIDDLE PATROCLUS]
Chiron passed away before I enlisted.

[MIDDLE ACHILLES]
That's not what I meant, Patroclus.

[MIDDLE PATROCLUS]
Then?

[MIDDLE ACHILLES]
I don't know. But losing him…it was hard on you.

[MIDDLE PATROCLUS]
We both lost him.

[MIDDLE ACHILLES]
That doesn't mean you didn't.

I just don't understand. You, of all people. You could go anywhere in the world, and you choose a heap of sand. The / great Patroclus!

[MIDDLE PATROCLUS]
/ A *wealthy* heap of sand. Greece has been looking for an excuse to sack Troy for ages.

[MIDDLE ACHILLES]
I don't understand the commotion. All this because a king's wife ran off with a Trojan / prince?

[MIDDLE PATROCLUS]
/ But that's not what it's really about. We'd gain full control of the sea, the allyship of the surrounding kingdoms—

[MIDDLE ACHILLES]
You sound like—

[MIDDLE PATROCLUS]
Like who?

[MIDDLE ACHILLES]
Like an old man.

[MIDDLE PATROCLUS]
Am I a distinguished one?

*Middle Achilles makes a noncommittal noise,
provoking indignation.*

All right. Where would I have gone, then?

[MIDDLE ACHILLES]
What?

[MIDDLE PATROCLUS]
If I weren't going to Troy.

[MIDDLE ACHILLES]
Pillars of Herakles.

[MIDDLE PATROCLUS]
Too far.

[MIDDLE ACHILLES]
Isle of Delos.

[MIDDLE PATROCLUS]
Too rocky.

[MIDDLE ACHILLES]
Home.

[MIDDLE PATROCLUS] *wry*
In case you've forgotten, my father made it very clear—

[MIDDLE ACHILLES]
I didn't mean there.

[MIDDLE PATROCLUS]
That's...that's your king / dom—

[MIDDLE ACHILLES]
/ We both—

[MIDDLE PATROCLUS]
You know how the Myrmidons look at me there.

[MIDDLE ACHILLES]
What do you / mean?

[MIDDLE PATROCLUS]
/ I was the child exile living on your father's grace.

[MIDDLE ACHILLES]
That's not true.

[MIDDLE PATROCLUS]
Yes, it is.

[MIDDLE ACHILLES]
They don't look at you that / way.

[MIDDLE PATROCLUS]
/ How would you know?

I have to go to Troy either way. I've sworn an oath to fight.

[MIDDLE ACHILLES]
I didn't know you felt that way.

[MIDDLE PATROCLUS]
That's your kingdom, Achilles. Not mine.

I didn't enlist because of Chiron.

[MIDDLE ACHILLES]
I wasn't sent to Mount Pelion because my mother died.

It is a subject that the two rarely, if ever, broach.

But I remember how it felt.

[MIDDLE PATROCLUS]
How did it feel?

[MIDDLE ACHILLES]
She was always watching me. Whether I was practicing my lyre, or playing in the trees with the other boys, or even at the big table at dinner. I could feel her eyes all day.

When I lost her, I felt bold. Like I could say or do whatever and it wouldn't matter. You can do anything, when nobody's watching.

Middle Patroclus looks away. And then he looks up again, staring steadily and unnervingly at Middle Achilles.

What are you doing?

[MIDDLE PATROCLUS]
Watching you. So you don't do anything.

[MIDDLE ACHILLES]
...you are *so*—

A playful fight that closes the space between them.

Middle Achilles leans back against a tree, pointing up at the sky and its rising constellations.

Look, Patroclus. The constellation Centaurus.

[MIDDLE PATROCLUS]
Where?

[MIDDLE ACHILLES]
Turn your head a little. No, the other way. This way. A little lower. Lower.

Middle Patroclus' head is now resting on Middle Achilles' shoulder.

[MIDDLE PATROCLUS] *teasing*
Soft.

Oh, I see it.

[MIDDLE ACHILLES]
Told you.

[MIDDLE PATROCLUS]
Right there.

[MIDDLE ACHILLES]
From now on, we'll always say that's him.

[MIDDLE PATROCLUS]
Who?

[MIDDLE ACHILLES]
Chiron, obviously.

[MIDDLE PATROCLUS]
Of course it is.

[MIDDLE ACHILLES]
Troy isn't that far away. He'll be there, too.

[MIDDLE PATROCLUS]
Good.

[MIDDLE ACHILLES]
Don't do anything I would do.

[MIDDLE PATROCLUS]
Like what?

[MIDDLE ACHILLES]

I don't know. Seize Troy, for instance.

[MIDDLE PATROCLUS]

Without you to watch me?

[MIDDLE ACHILLES]

Careful, Patroclus. You just might persuade me to come with you.

Was that a joke? Middle Patroclus decides that it is.

[MIDDLE PATROCLUS]

I'll do what I've sworn to do. I'll bring the runaway queen back to Greece.

[MIDDLE ACHILLES]

Then...?

[MIDDLE PATROCLUS]

Then you'll be sitting on your throne. Back at your father's house. Your queen will be at your side. She's lovely, wise. A messenger will enter, announcing that a friend is here to see you. You'll say, "Bring him in." And you wait. But you already know who it is. A soldier steps into the hall, dressed in glittering armor. He's older, but otherwise the same as you remember him. He smiles. Or tries to. Mostly, he just looks at you. Finally, he says...

Anticipation.

"Still no beard?"

Indignation. Triumph. The two break into laughter.

[MIDDLE ACHILLES]
It's coming in.

[MIDDLE PATROCLUS]
All right.

A playful attack.

Tell it to hurry up, then. You're a man now.

[MIDDLE ACHILLES]
You, too?

[MIDDLE PATROCLUS]
What?

[MIDDLE ACHILLES]
My father's been saying that. I hate it. I feel so behind.

[MIDDLE PATROCLUS]
You?

[MIDDLE ACHILLES]
Doesn't everyone? We look around, we see the world moving faster than we are, and we run as fast as we can so we aren't left behind. We're all just...we're scared into it all.

[MIDDLE PATROCLUS]
You call me the philosophical one.

[MIDDLE ACHILLES]
I'm catching up.

[MIDDLE PATROCLUS]
Are you?

[MIDDLE ACHILLES]
I learned from the best.

[MIDDLE PATROCLUS]
Hm.

Middle Patroclus rises and reaches down to help Middle Achilles up. Lights up on present-day Achilles and Patroclus in their tent. It's early morning. Achilles had been sleeping. Patroclus slips in.

[ACHILLES] *waking*
Patroclus?

[PATROCLUS]
Sorry.

[ACHILLES]
When did you get back?

[PATROCLUS]
You were dead asleep, Endymion. I didn't mean to wake you.

For the first time, Patroclus smiles genuinely, but there is something secret about that smile that makes Achilles afraid.

[ACHILLES]
You're—smiling.

[PATROCLUS]
Does Prince Achilles forbid me to smile?

[ACHILLES]
Can I guess what you're thinking?

[PATROCLUS]
No, you can't.

Achilles is encouraged by Patroclus' good mood, even if he doesn't understand the secret it contains.

[ACHILLES]
You'll tell me soon enough. You always do.

[PATROCLUS]
It's still dark out. Go back to sleep, Achilles.

Lights on Middle Achilles and Middle Patroclus, as well.

[MIDDLE ACHILLES]
It's nighttime, Patroclus.

[MIDDLE PATROCLUS]
It's still evening, Achilles.

The past and the present weave together.

[ACHILLES]
I'm awake.

[MIDDLE ACHILLES]
The stars are out, the moon is up—

[MIDDLE PATROCLUS]
Because it's evening, Achilles.

[MIDDLE ACHILLES]
Then how do you want to spend the *evening*, Patro / clus?

[ACHILLES]
/ How do you want to spend the day, Patroclus?

[MIDDLE PATROCLUS]
With you.

[MIDDLE ACHILLES]
You've been doing that all day.

[PATROCLUS & MIDDLE PATROCLUS]
Doesn't matter.

In the past, an affectionate gesture from Middle Achilles to Middle Patroclus. In the present, Patroclus' secret smile returns.

[MIDDLE ACHILLES]
Let's get some sleep. What would Chiron say?

[MIDDLE PATROCLUS]
No.

[MIDDLE ACHILLES]
Come on, old man. What would Chiron say? What would Chiron say?

[PATROCLUS & MIDDLE PATROCLUS]
There's always tomorrow.

Drumming rolls up from the orchestra. The Soldiers Ensemble pours in, sweeping Middle Patroclus and Middle Achilles offstage.

IX

ASHES LIKE STARS

A small distance from Achilles and Patroclus' tent, the Soldiers Ensemble is locked in bitter combat. Patroclus rises abruptly, hiding his expression. He exits the tent, going towards the fighting with the dazed, unquestioning certainty of a man in a dream. As he does, the sounds of battle grow louder.

[ACHILLES] *calling after him*
Patroclus? Patroclus!

Low rumbles of underscoring. The walls of space dissolve, and all the action of the following scene happens in vignettes in the midst of the battle-locked ensemble. First, in a small pocket of light, Patroclus spies Phoenix rising, reaching for a spear. He goes swiftly to him, pushes the old man gently down onto a stool.

[PATROCLUS]
Phoenix, what are you doing?

[PHOENIX]
I have to help them.

[PATROCLUS]

Sit down, Phoenix.

[PHOENIX]

Let me go.

[PATROCLUS]

Phoenix, please.

[PHOENIX]

I can fight.

[PATROCLUS]

I know. I know you can. But not yet. You have to save your strength for when they need you most.

Phoenix at last collapses into the seat more out of exhaustion than acquiescence.

Do you want anything? Water? Wine?

[PHOENIX]

I should be out there.

[PATROCLUS]

I know.

[PHOENIX]

I led charges in my youth, only to be left with no strength when I need it.

[PATROCLUS]

Let me pour you a drink.

[PHOENIX]

What use? We'll all be feasts for dogs by end of day.

[PATROCLUS]

All our best soldiers are out there. They'll protect—

[PHOENIX]

Protect with what? Their lives?

[PATROCLUS]

He won't relent until—

[PHOENIX]

He'll win his honor but enjoy it alone.

[PATROCLUS]

Let me see what I can do. Maybe I can talk—

[PHOENIX]

Is this the Achilles we know?

Talthybius fights through the crowd, bursts into Phoenix's pocket of light.

[TALTHYBIUS]

Patroclus. I've been looking everywhere.

[PATROCLUS]

I was going to speak with Achilles. What's happened?

[TALTHYBIUS]

A dozen wounded men are asking for you.

[PATROCLUS]

What about the healer?

[TALTHYBIUS]

He's one of them.

[PATROCLUS]

The other medics?

[TALTHYBIUS]

All fighting Hector off. We needed
every man we could get.

Patroclus is already gathering supplies from around Phoenix's tent.

[PATROCLUS]

I'll be back soon, Phoenix. I promise.

[PHOENIX]

It's like his mother once told you. He follows where you lead.
So lead him, Patroclus.

*With a final look back at Phoenix, Patroclus follows Talthybius out,
and the lights on Phoenix fade. The spotlight next finds them halfway
across the stage, lurchingly intercepted by a wounded Ajax.*

[AJAX]
Patroclus!

[PATROCLUS]
There. You're all right.

Patroclus catches Ajax as he stumbles and lowers him carefully to the ground.

[AJAX]
Where the hell have you been? We've all been asking for you.

[PATROCLUS]
I hope I can live up to the welcome.

He looks to Talthybius.

If you'll give me a moment?

[TALTHYBIUS]
I have to report back. I'll come find you again.

[PATROCLUS]
Bring me whatever medical supplies you can find. I'll need them.

Talthybius runs and disappears offstage. Patroclus kneels by Ajax.

Let's see what we have here.

He inspects the wound and immediately starts his work.

[AJAX]
You were always Chiron's favorite, back on Mount Pelion.

[PATROCLUS]
I wouldn't say that, Ajax.

[AJAX]
Well, let's see if those healing lessons did us any good.

Remember in spring? We'd take our lessons outside?

[PATROCLUS]
That spot under the trees outside the cave.

[AJAX]
Fig trees, olive trees—

Patroclus speaks as soothingly as possible in order to distract the wounded man from what he is about to do.

[PATROCLUS]
Rivers, fresh springs. Forests. The smell of springtime pears from up the mountain. A wind that never sounds lonely. And as the days got colder, when you went up to the heights, even gentle snowfall—

[AJAX] *a cry of intense pain*
Ahh!

[PATROCLUS]
There. You're all right. I've got it. The worst is over.

He begins to apply a salve.

[AJAX] *in intense pain*
Trained by a healer known for gentleness. And yet the cruelest man I know.

[PATROCLUS]
I didn't mean to hurt / you—

[AJAX]
/ Not you. I wasn't talking about you. How could Achilles do this to us? Ten years in battle together, growing up together on Mount Pelion, and he leaves us to die? Just because of some Trojan slave girl?

[PATROCLUS]
You know it's not about Briseis.

[AJAX]
Then just because he's scared?

Ajax is attempting to stand. Patroclus reaches to stay him.

[PATROCLUS]
Sit down.

[AJAX]
I have to report back.

[PATROCLUS]
No, you don't. You've lost too much blood.

[AJAX]
I'll die if I go, die if I stay. And I'm not the only one. Give me
my spear.

*A deeply conflicted Patroclus hands it to him. Ajax rises and staggers
off. The spotlight finds Talthybius pushing through the mass, his arms
full of medical supplies.*

[TALTHYBIUS]
Patroclus—

[PATROCLUS]
Odysseus. I need to find Odysseus.

[TALTHYBIUS]
Patroclus—

*Patroclus is already running offstage, leaving Talthybius standing.
The relentless images of battle continue, sweeping the scene to a separate
part of camp: Agamemnon's tent. When Patroclus runs back onstage, he
nearly runs into a bloodied Agamemnon, who has just earned his own
pocket of light.*

[PATROCLUS]
Sir? What's happened?

[AGAMEMNON]
Take a single guess.

[PATROCLUS]
Sir, Achilles won't budge. You're the only one—

[AGAMEMNON]

I just tried.

[PATROCLUS]

You did?

[AGAMEMNON]

If you aren't going to help us, then at least stay out of my way.

[PATROCLUS]

Let me bandage that, sir.

[AGAMEMNON]

You're the last person I want laying hands on my wounds.

Agamemnon begins to stagger offstage, then calls:

The *second* last.

He exits. Patroclus begins to rush off when Briseis steps quickly into the light, intercepting him.

[BRISEIS]

Sir.

[PATROCLUS]

Briseis.

[BRISEIS]

I heard your voice last night. I couldn't come out.

They speak in hushed voices, even as the roar of battle grows louder.

[PATROCLUS]

Agamemnon hasn't hurt you?

[BRISEIS]

What use are dirty goods for bargaining?

What are you doing in camp?

[PATROCLUS]

We aren't fighting. Achilles won't fight.

The noises of battle grow more urgent, more present, with every passing moment.

[BRISEIS]

Achilles won't fight for you, even though the ships will burn?

[PATROCLUS]

He knows he won't be going home either way.

[BRISEIS]

It isn't just him.

[PATROCLUS]

Briseis, I need to find Odysseus.

[BRISEIS]

Odysseus?

[PATROCLUS]
Have you seen him? Do you know if he—

A great thundering sound as the wall is breached. Shouts of terror and triumph rise. Talthybius runs up to the two.

[TALTHYBIUS]
The wall.

[PATROCLUS]
They're here?

[TALTHYBIUS]
Ajax is holding them.

[PATROCLUS]
And who else?

Talthybius' look tells Patroclus what he needs to know.

[TALTHYBIUS]
He's strong, but he isn't Achilles. He won't last long.

We need you defending the camp, Patroclus. You, and every Myrmidon you can muster.

[PATROCLUS]
I'm not—The Myrmidons don't answer to me.

[TALTHYBIUS]
And I'm not much of a soldier,

but I'm wise enough to fight for my life.

With that, Talthybius grabs whatever weapons he can find and runs off, arming himself as he goes.

"The Slave Women's Lament" theme plays, a cold, lonely sound that nevertheless offers stillness amidst the chaos. Briseis pulls a decorative dagger from the folds of her dress.

[BRISEIS]
Take this, sir.

[PATROCLUS]
I don't need weapons.

[BRISEIS]
It isn't one. There's my family sigil. You don't look much like the other Myrmidons. Maybe without the helmet, my people will not know you. When they take the camp, say you are a captive. Say you serve the house of Princess Briseis of Lyrnessus. I will come for you.

[PATROCLUS]
Why me?

[BRISEIS]
Of all the men, you were always kind to me.

She makes a series of shapes with her hands. Patroclus echoes them with his own—then presses the dagger back into her hands.

[PATROCLUS]
Keep it, Briseis.

[BRISEIS]
They'll slaughter everyone. It's your only hope.

[PATROCLUS]
No matter what happens, you'll be safe. Agamemnon will bring you back to us and we'll take you to Greece.

[BRISEIS]
What are you talking about?

[PATROCLUS]
We'll take you back to Achilles' father. You'll live there in his house. You'll have a good life.

[BRISEIS]
My people have won.

[PATROCLUS]
One way or another, Achilles will fight.

By now, Trojans are pouring into the camp with torches. As Patroclus tears himself away, the Soldiers Ensemble crowds around him, men limping, men carrying their comrades, men crawling on the ground, in nightmare choreography. The "Cleopatra" theme rises over the relentless, feverish percussion. Patroclus fights his way through the melee, tries to tend to whoever he can, but there is nowhere for him to turn.

Just like the mythic Cleopatra, Patroclus runs through the masses of the dying and dead back to his beloved. He exits.

X

WHO IS THIS BOY?

A deeply agitated Patroclus is talking with Achilles at their tent.

[ACHILLES]

All I asked for was my honor. I was going to give my life for Agamem / non.

[PATROCLUS]

/ Stop saying Agamemnon. This isn't about him. This is about all the men who have died, who are dying right now, because of you. Because you won't fight today.

[ACHILLES]

Patroclus, none of us have to die for him.

[PATROCLUS]

Of course we don't. But you made your choice ten years ago.

[ACHILLES]

And I won't give them any more than I already have.

[PATROCLUS]
You have nothing left to give them.

Say Agamemnon came right now with all the gifts and
promises in the world. It wouldn't change a thing. We're never
getting back the life you threw away, Achilles.

[ACHILLES]
Patroclus, if I could have just one more day—

[PATROCLUS]
Don't—

[ACHILLES]
Back on Mount Pelion with—

[PATROCLUS]
This isn't about us.

[ACHILLES]
It should have been.

[PATROCLUS]
But it's not. Not anymore.

[ACHILLES]
Please don't keep saying that.

[PATROCLUS]
When have I—?

[ACHILLES]

You are the one who—you—you never bring up the stories we had. I want to say anything about those people and those places—I start to talk about Chiron, and you change the subject. Or you look away. And it kills me.

[PATROCLUS]

We can't go back there.

[ACHILLES]

So I remember it. I remember it.

[PATROCLUS]

You think I don't?

[ACHILLES]

It seems like you want to forget it.

[PATROCLUS]

It seems like you didn't want it.

[ACHILLES]

Patroclus, I always wanted—

[PATROCLUS]

I watch you waking up, and cleaning up our dinner, and hiding behind your hair when you smile, and I grieve you more every time I see you.

[ACHILLES]

I know. I *know*. But just because I won't be here

tomorrow doesn't mean I'm not here now. Can you just ac-knowledge that we lived? That I live?

[PATROCLUS]
I grieve our future every day. I don't have the heart to grieve our past, as well.

[ACHILLES]
Patroclus.

[PATROCLUS]
WHO IS THIS BOY? HIS NOISE AND HIS DANGER
YOUR VIOLENCE GLEAMS, YOU'RE DAZED WITH
SILENT DREAMS
AND MOONLIGHT MADE YOU SEEM A STRANGER

I KNOW A BOY. I'VE KNOWN HIM FOREVER
BUT THERE'S A DAY WHEN HE TURNED BACK TO
LOOK AT ME
AND SOMEONE ELSE WAS IN HIS ARMOR

WE'VE GROWN TOO BRAVE FOR PRETENDING
I KNOW YOUR LIFE'S NOT MINE TO SAVE
WE'RE RACING LIKE A HEARTBEAT TO THE ENDING
SO JUST LET ME TRY TO SAVE MY HEART FROM
BREAKING

YOU'RE RESTLESS, I'M QUIET
EACH GLANCE IS A QUESTION
AND SUNRISE IS FALLING
LIKE ASH FROM THE HEAVENS

[ACHILLES]
WHO IS THIS BOY? HE'S PANICKED, DEFIANT
NOW HE STANDS ALONE, IS THIS THE PRINCE I'D
KNOWN?
HOW CAN I DENY HIM?

[PATROCLUS]
IS THIS THE BOY WHO NO MAN CAN FRIGHTEN?
IN THE CHILL OF DAWN, ALL HIS DEFENSES GONE
AND SO LIKE A CHILD AGAIN

IN OTHER DAYS
WE WERE BENDING TOWARD THE SUN
LIKE A BOWSTRING YIELDS TO LET ITS ARROWS
BLAZE
WE'RE RACING DOWN THE HILLSIDE AND IT FEELS
SO LONG AGO, UNREAL, AND I CAN'T HELP THE ACHE

AND SWIFTLY I'M FALLING THROUGH
TIME LIKE AN ARROW
THE STRING BREAKS, THE BIRD FLIES
AND MEMORY IS FREEDOM

WHO IS THIS BOY?
I DON'T THINK I KNOW THIS BOY

If you don't fight today—

[ACHILLES]
I gave up everything for them, and I will get every last thing
they promised me. Should I let Agamemnon humiliate me?

Should I die for him and let him have my honor, too? We've
taken it this far. I won't bend now.

[PATROCLUS]
Then I will.

[ACHILLES]
What?

[PATROCLUS]
Dress me in your armor and let me fight in your stead. You
won't have to serve Agamemnon or give in to the prophecy. The
Trojans will take me for you, and the Myrmidons will chase them
from the ships, and our people will be saved.

[ACHILLES]
You'll get yourself killed.

[PATROCLUS]
We'll give the Trojans a scare, that's all. There's no prophecy
over my head. We'll push them out of the camp, be back by afternoon—

[ACHILLES]
Patroclus—

[PATROCLUS]
Think of what you said to me that day by the river on Mount
Pelion. You said—

[ACHILLES] *bittersweetly, like friends over an old joke*
WHAT IF THE GODS COULD CHANGE YOU?

[PATROCLUS]
YOU TRIED TO SPEAK

[ACHILLES / PATROCLUS]
BUT I COULDN'T / BUT YOU COULDN'T

[PATROCLUS]
AND YOU BLINKED TWICE

[ACHILLES]
AND I SAID TO YOU

[PATROCLUS / ACHILLES]
THAT YOU WOULD GROW WITH ME / I WOULD
GROW WITH YOU

YOU SWORE THAT YOU WOULD GO WITH ME,
ACHILLES / HOWEVER WE'RE CHANGING

AND YOU SAID YOU'D BE HERE TOMORROW / I'LL BE
WITH YOU ALWAYS

[PATROCLUS]
YOU'VE ALWAYS HAD MY LOVE
AND SINCE THAT'S NOT ENOUGH
WHERE YOU ARE GOING, LET ME FOLLOW

WE'VE GROWN TOO BRAVE FOR PRETENDING

I KNOW THAT YOU'RE NOT MINE TO SAVE
WE'RE RACING LIKE A HEARTBEAT TO THE ENDING
SO JUST LET ME TRY—

So just let me *try*.

[ACHILLES] *haltingly*
DON'T TAKE TROY WITHOUT ME
I'LL DO THE REST
WE'LL HAVE OUR FOREVER

[PATROCLUS]
OR WHATEVER IS LEFT

Let me go, Achilles.

[ACHILLES]
Then you will return to me?

Patroclus nods. Achilles hesitates, searching Patroclus' face. He nods assent.

[ACHILLES]
WERE WE THE BOYS

[ACHILLES & PATROCLUS]
WHO WERE GODS FOR A MOMENT?

[PATROCLUS]
YOU WERE BORN DIVINE, BUT YOU WEREN'T SATIS-
FIED

ACHILLES HAD TO BE A HERO

[ACHILLES]
TEN YEARS AGO
WE WATCHED AND WE WONDERED
THE WORLD WAS YOUNG
OUR LIVES A SONG UNSUNG
YOUR EYES THE DROWSY SHADE OF SUMMER

[PATROCLUS]
I'VE GROWN TOO BRAVE FOR PRETENDING
BUT THEN THE DARKNESS MEETS
YOUR DEATHLESS GAZE
IT FEELS LIKE THIS WILL BE A BRIGHT FOREVER
MEMORY'S LIKE A DREAM AND I'M SO CLOSE TO
WAKING

[ACHILLES]
WE LAY BY THE RIVER
THE SUNLIGHT WAS BREATHLESS

[PATROCLUS]
WE'RE QUIET

[ACHILLES]
WE'RE RESTLESS

[PATROCLUS]
EACH GLANCE WAS A QUESTION

[ACHILLES & PATROCLUS]
WHO IS THIS BOY?
WHO IS THIS BOY?
WHO IS THIS BOY?
I THINK THAT I LOVE THIS BOY

Their figures are so human that they are almost immortal.

XI

ARISTEIA

*M*usic. Patroclus emerges from the tent, resplendent in Achilles' armor. More and more soldiers gather around him. He is dizzy with hope, perhaps even senseless with it.

As the soldiers charge into the field, the captives emerge from their tents, bearing silent witness. Briseis is among them, finally understanding what Patroclus was planning to do.

Lights shift. The ranks swell. Patroclus stands atop his chariot, the battle swirling around him in dreamlike choreography. He lifts his spear.

He blazes with his own sudden grace, felling man after man. The Trojans scatter in terror at his advance. And, as the walls of Troy approach, he leaps off and begins to scale them.

This quasi dream sequence turns nightmare as Patroclus falls. His helmet is dislodged, exposing him for all to see. Enraged at the deception, the Trojans crowd around him. For a moment, Patroclus circles like a trapped animal—and then plunges himself back into the fighting.

He is pierced in the back by a Trojan soldier and stumbles backwards into the ranks of the Greeks. The crowd of Trojans parts, and Hector himself emerges from the melee, resplendent in his quiet dignity. He spears Patroclus in the stomach. Crying out in pain, Patroclus stumbles to the ground as the soldiers vocalize around him.

Patroclus takes his last breath. Odysseus and Ajax guard Patroclus' body; surrounded by Greek soldiers, Odysseus begins to carry it back to the beach.

As the crowd clears, we see Achilles, gazing anxiously out at the battlefield.

Odysseus, Ajax, and Phoenix slowly make their way towards him.

Achilles sinks to his knees.

A heartbeat drum that fades into silence.

Intermission.

ACT II:
ACHILLES

XII

O ICARUS

*I*t is afternoon. Achilles stands in front of his tent, waiting. In the background, barely noticeable, Iphis and Diomede go about their duties, but they, too, are restless.

Patroclus, still in his bloodstained battle garb, appears in a spotlight downstage. He begins singing in silence, punctuated by drumbeats and light chords; just one or two other instruments eventually enter, accompanying the song sparsely.

[PATROCLUS]
TWO KINGS WALKING
DOWN THE STRAND
THEIR SHOULDERS HUNCH
THEIR SHIRTS ARE TORN

Odysseus enters, bearing the body of Patroclus. Phoenix is with him. Ajax trails after, dazed and devastated, carrying the spoils of war Patroclus had won that day.

ONE MAN LIMPING

ONE MAN GRIM
SOMETHING CRADLED
IN THEIR ARMS

NOW THEY'RE COMING
HE LOOKS ON
ONE MORE MOMENT
ONE MORE BREATH

THEN GOLDEN FEATHERS
TOUCH THE GROUND
HE TEARS HIS HAIR
WHO MADE THIS MESS?

As Achilles falls to his knees and tears his hair out, the men all come to his side.

HE CRIES MY NAME
HE MAKES NO SOUND
O ICARUS
IS FALLING FAST

[ODYSSEUS] *simultaneously, ad lib until next chord*
/ Achilles--Achilles, listen to me. Put down your weapon. That's it. Look at me. Look at me now, Achilles.

[PHOENIX] *simultaneously, ad lib until next chord*
/ Oh, my prince. My prince. Achilles, listen to him. Achilles, Achilles, my prince.

[**AJAX**] *simultaneously, ad lib until next chord*
/ We tried to stop him. He insisted on pressing on towards
Troy. We tried. We tried. We tried.

[ODYSSEUS]
THE MEN ARE CLOSE
WE STAY HIS HAND

[PHOENIX]
HE KNOCKS US DOWN

[AJAX]
WE'RE ON THE FLOOR

The faint sounds of Odysseus talking to Achilles, of Achilles' incoherent responses.

[PATROCLUS]
YET ONE MAN SEEMS
TO UNDERSTAND

[AJAX]
HE PLEADS WITH HIM

[PHOENIX]
IT'S LIKE BEFORE

Ajax and Phoenix begin talking, too, and their voices grow in volume. Over the continued murmuring, Briseis enters, accompanied by Agamemnon and Talthybius, carrying rich gifts for Achilles. They all stop short at the scene that greets them.

[AGAMEMNON] *to Talthybius*
THE GIRL CAN GO

[BRISEIS]
I HEED THE MAN
WHAT GAME THEY PLAY
I CANNOT SEE

*The tent drapes flutter in the wind, revealing Achilles' crumpled
form. Briseis understands all.*

THE CURTAINS BLOW
I SEE HIM THEN

[PATROCLUS]
THE TRUTH BETRAYED

[BRISEIS & PATROCLUS]
IT CANNOT BE

*Even if Briseis were capable of movement in that moment, she would
not have been let through. She stands apart from the rest, watching.
Odysseus, Ajax, and Phoenix hum softly under Patroclus, while Briseis'
voice rises in a high, unheard cry of despair.*

[PATROCLUS]
AND IT'S LIKE SOME STORY
TOLD TO ME
I'VE HEARD THIS SONG
I KNOW IT WELL

AND THIS MOMENT SEEMS
LIKE MEMORY
IT'S DUST IN SUNLIGHT
BREATH MEETS AIR

AND I STILL BELIEVE THAT
I'M STILL HERE
AND I'M GRIEVING, BREATHING
AND THE GRIEF IS AIR

SO TAKE MY BREATHS
THEY CATCH THE BREEZE
O ICARUS
YOUR LOVELY WINGS

THEIR HEARTS BEAT FAST
THOSE FRAGILE THINGS
O ICARUS
YOUR LOVELY WINGS

*Lights fade out swiftly on the final note,
as if someone is closing their eyes.*

XIII

VISITATIONS

E*vening. On one or two instruments, an echo of the "O Icarus" melody plays faintly through the scene transition and carries over into this scene.*

The tent wall is up, and in silhouette, we see Achilles again grieving by Patroclus' side. The figures of Phoenix, Odysseus, and Ajax are all around Achilles, each offering silent, unheard words of comfort and sorrow. He does not let them take the body.

They exit, taking down the tent wall as they do. Lights shift to night, dark and dreamy, and Achilles walks slowly down the beach. He sits and stares out at the water. The ensemble supplies the sound of ocean waves.

Enter Thetis, in a surreal cast of light. Her voice is softer than before, entreating.

[THETIS]
ACHILLEUS, WILL YOU NOT HEED?
COME AWAY FROM THE SIGHT OF THE SLAUGHTER

TURN YOUR FACE FROM THE THINGS
THAT WERE TAKEN
THEY HAVE FINALLY PAID FOR YOUR HONOR

WILL YOU NOT HEED?
WILL YOU NOT HEED?
WILL YOU NOT HEED?

ARISTOS
ARISTOS ACHAION

She reaches out to touch him. He turns away as Patroclus enters,
bloodied.

[PATROCLUS]
WHO IS THIS BOY?
HE'S STRICKEN, HE'S BROKEN
IN THE VIOLET MOONLIGHT, LET US LEAVE THIS
ROOM
FOR FAR TOO SOON YOU'LL BE AWOKEN

YOU'VE GROWN TOO BRAVE FOR PRETENDING
THERE'S NOTHING LEFT FOR YOU TO SAVE
JUST SWEAR YOU'LL LET OUR ASHES LIE TOGETHER
AND I'LL MEET YOU IN THE GOLDEN LIGHT OF DAY

Achilles springs to his feet as Patroclus retreats. Thetis intercepts
Achilles as he rushes after him.

[PATROCLUS / THETIS]
WHO IS THIS BOY? / ACHILLEUS

WHO IS THIS BOY? / ACHILLEUS
WHO IS THIS BOY? / ACHILLEUS
WHO IS THIS BOY? / ACHILLEUS

Patroclus exits. Music underscores the ensuing dialogue.

[THETIS]

Have you eaten?

Have you slept?

Achilles, sit down.

[ACHILLES]

Hector did this to him.

[THETIS]

Achilles, let Agamemnon go against Hector. This isn't your battle. This isn't your war.

[ACHILLES]

Hector still lives.

[THETIS]

Achilles, listen to me. Enough blood has been shed in this meaningless fight. Don't let another father mourn his son.

I left my home and all my sisters. I went to your father's kingdom. I endured that throne and that marriage bed so you would be a prince, not the bastard child of a powerless woman. But if you do this, I won't be able to protect you any longer.

Remember, Achilles, if you slay Hector...

[ACHILLES]
I missed you all my life.

[THETIS]
I know.

[ACHILLES]
I'm glad I lost you, sometimes.

[THETIS]
Why?

[ACHILLES]
So you never had to lose me.

The electric guitar starts up in choppy, agitated phrases.

[THETIS]
I won't lose you, Achilles.

[ACHILLES]
When Hector dies...

[THETIS]
Hector will live.

[ACHILLES]
Hector killed him.

[THETIS]
You will live.

[ACHILLES]
We always knew I would die here.

[THETIS]
It didn't need to be this way, Achilles.

[ACHILLES]
Didn't it?

[THETIS]
You never had to come here.

[ACHILLES]
What else could I have been?

[THETIS]
Oh, your father hoped you'd exceed him. He was one hero among many, forgotten in a generation, and he wanted his son to be a legend. But you didn't need to do this. The gods gave you everything I never had. They gave you a choice.

Thetis' theme returns now as a dark ballad, accompanied by percussion and electric guitar.

ACHILLEUS
LOOK AT YOU NOW
YOU'RE SWEATING AND BLEEDING AND CRYING
YOU'RE WASTING AND ROTTING AND DYING

ACHILLEUS
PELEUS' SON
DO YOU KNOW ALL MY SORROW IS FOR YOU?
DO YOU KNOW WHAT I BORE AS I BORE YOU?
DID I GIVE YOU MY WORLD JUST TO MOURN YOU?

I HAD KNOWN THAT YOUR LIFE
WOULD BE FLEETING
YET YOU DOOM YOURSELF TWICE WITH YOUR
GRIEVING
WOULD YOU CAST AWAY ALL THAT I GAVE YOU?
WOULD YOU SNEER AT THE ONE WHO WOULD SAVE
YOU?

WHO IS THIS BOY?
WHO IS THIS MONSTER?
I GAVE YOU FOREVER
AND THIS IS WHAT YOU WANTED?

As "Who Is This Boy?" pulses electric in the orchestra, Thetis exits, leaving Achilles alone on the beach. Lights snap out over the raging of the guitar.

The dream is over, but the nightmare continues. The music rages on. Achilles emerges from his tent to find a glistening set of new armor on a rack. He dresses. He tips headlong into an unearthly scream. The lights shift rapidly, dark and surreal. The guitar ascends dizzyingly. Jagged shards of war. Achilles slaughters Trojan after Trojan. At last, he kills Hector, but this is only the beginning. The Greeks look on, appalled, even scared. Achilles mutilates the body, dragging it all the way home. Carnage. Horror. Heavy rock. Inhuman, animal, godlike rage.

And then quiet.

And then quiet.

XIV

THE SLAVE WOMEN'S LAMENT

A chilles' tent. Flanked by Iphis and Diomede, Briseis washes the body of Patroclus. She hums the first verse of the melody.

[BRISEIS]
HMM...

On the second verse, Iphis and Diomede join in, and the three sing on an open vowel.

[BRISEIS, IPHIS, & DIOMEDE]
AHH...

[IPHIS]
SO PICK A FIGHT
SO CALL ON HELL
SO BLAME IT ON SOME GIRL

[DIOMEDE]
HER LOVER'S PISSED
AND JUST AS WELL
YOU SNATCH HIS BRONZE AND PEARLS

[IPHIS]
WHO TELLS OF HOW WE SUFFERED?
WHO SINGS ABOUT OUR LAUGHTER?
WE BUILD OUR FIRES
THERE IS NO AFTER

[DIOMEDE]
WE'VE HEARD YOUR PEOPLE'S STORIES
YOU CALL US WIVES AND DAUGHTERS
BY ANCIENT PYRES
WE GRIEVE THE SLAUGHTER
WE CRY LAMENTS TO MAKE YOU HEAR

[IPHIS]
WE SING YOUR GRIEF TO MAKE YOU HEAR

[DIOMEDE]
WE RISE LIKE SMOKE AND DISAPPEAR

[IPHIS & DIOMEDE]
AND GRIEF GIVES WAY TO
GRIEF GIVES WAY TO
GRIEF GIVES WAY TO GRIEF

The orchestra ramps up to an unrelenting tempo, the lament exploding into a rock number.

[IPHIS]
WE CAME SO FAR

[DIOMEDE]
WE BEAR THE SCARS

[IPHIS]
BUT THE GLORY'S YOURS TO KEEP

[BRISEIS]
SO YOU'LL SAY THE HERO LOVED HIM
MORE THAN ANYBODY ELSE DID
MY HEART WAS BROKEN
BUT HOW I FELT IT
THE GENTLE GRIEF WHEN HE WAS NEAR

NOW ALL THAT'S LEFT ARE ASHES
YOU WILL BURN HIM DOWN TO ASHES
I GRASP AT NOTHING
AT TIME IN SNATCHES
THE MOMENT SNAPS AND NOW THE MAN APPEARS

Achilles, in bloody war gear, enters from behind Briseis. A ragged crowd of Captives gathers around the pair and quietly takes up the chant under the dialogue.

[ACHILLES]
Make room.

[BRISEIS]
You killed Hector?

[ACHILLES]
I dragged him through the dust.

[BRISEIS]
For what?

[ACHILLES]
He'll pay for what he's done.

[BRISEIS]
It wasn't Hector who did this.

[IPHIS, DIOMEDE, & CAPTIVES] *sotto voce*
GRIEF GIVES WAY TO
GRIEF GIVES WAY TO
GRIEF GIVES WAY TO GRIEF

[BRISEIS]
SO YOU SAT RIGHT HERE
AND SMILED GOODBYE
AND SENT HIM OFF TO DIE?

[ACHILLES]
I couldn't have said no to him. Do you know how hard I tried?

[BRISEIS]
YOU'RE NO DIFFERENT THAN THE REST OF THEM
YOU TRIED TO SELL ME FOR YOUR PRIDE
BUT OF COURSE THAT WASN'T GOOD ENOUGH
SO YOU RAN AND TOOK YOUR FLIGHT
AND YOU DRESSED HIM UP TO FIGHT

YOU WENT AND SOLD HIS LIFE

[BRISEIS, IPHIS, DIOMEDE, & CAPTIVES]
AND GRIEF GIVES WAY TO
GRIEF GIVES WAY TO
GRIEF GIVES WAY TO GRIEF

[BRISEIS / IPHIS, DIOMEDE, & CAPTIVES]
YOU WANTED THIS / AND GRIEF GIVES WAY TO
YOU'D DIE FOR THIS / GRIEF GIVES WAY TO
AND NOW YOU DARE TO WEEP? / GRIEF GIVES WAY
TO GRIEF

[BRISEIS]
THE DAY HE HAD ENOUGH OF IT
HE FOLLOWED WHERE YOU LED
IT'S TOUCHING
ALL THIS LOVE FOR HIM
BUT HE'S ALREADY DEAD

WHERE'S YOUR HONOR, WHERE'S YOUR HONESTY?
WHERE'D YOUR COURAGE GO TO HIDE?
AND WE ALL WERE SURE YOU LOVED HIM
NOW WE ALL KNOW THAT YOU LIED
WHERE'S YOUR DARLING GOLDEN PRIDE?
WHERE WERE YOU WHEN HE DIED?

[IPHIS, DIOMEDE, & CAPTIVES] *increasing in volume*
AND GRIEF GIVES WAY TO
GRIEF GIVES WAY TO
GRIEF GIVES WAY TO GRIEF

AND GRIEF GIVES WAY TO
GRIEF GIVES WAY TO
GRIEF GIVES WAY TO GRIEF…

[BRISEIS / IPHIS, DIOMEDE, & CAPTIVES]
YOU'D GO AND FIGHT A WAR FOR STRANGERS /
GRIEF GIVES WAY TO
BUT YOU WON'T FIGHT FOR YOUR BELOVED / GRIEF
GIVES WAY TO GRIEF
YOU SIT HERE SAFE AND PROUD AND PRECIOUS /
GRIEF GIVES WAY TO
WHILE PATROCLUS DIES ALONE / GRIEF GIVES WAY
TO GRIEF

[IPHIS & DIOMEDE]
THE MOMENT OF OUR FATE HAS COME

[BRISEIS, IPHIS, DIOMEDE, & CAPTIVES]
AND MAY OUR LIVES BE BRIEF

[BRISEIS]
'CAUSE YOU LEFT YOUR HALLOWED CITY
AND IT WASN'T EVEN BURNING
A THOUSAND SHIPS
AN OCEAN CHURNING
YOU DOOMED A THOUSAND LIVES AND THEN

AGAIN THE END WILL COME
AGAIN THE WALLS WILL CRUMBLE
THERE WILL BE SMOKE
THERE WILL BE THUNDER

THE HUNGRY FLAMES WILL CRAWL AGAIN

[BRISEIS, IPHIS, DIOMEDE, & CAPTIVES]
GRIEF GIVES WAY TO
GRIEF GIVES WAY TO
GRIEF GIVES WAY TO GRIEF

GRIEF GIVES WAY TO
GRIEF GIVES WAY TO
GRIEF GIVES WAY TO GRIEF

GRIEF GIVES WAY TO
GRIEF GIVES WAY TO
GRIEF GIVES WAY TO GRIEF

GRIEF GIVES WAY TO
GRIEF GIVES WAY TO
GRIEF GIVES WAY TO GRIEF

[BRISEIS] *turning to Achilles*
YOU CAME THIS FAR
HE BEARS THE SCARS
THE GLORY'S YOURS TO KEEP

XV

PRIAM

*I*t is night. Ajax and Talthybius are outside Achilles' tent, squatting in the dirt and playing dice to pass the time. Briseis, Iphis, and Diomede are visible in the background, silently cleaning up the firepit after dinner.*

[AJAX]

Tying him to his chariot. Dragging him around the walls of Troy. It's not...I mean, I've got no love for the Trojans.

[TALTHYBIUS]

Of course.

[AJAX]

But even they wouldn't dare. You kill a man, you take his armor, you let his comrades bring home the body. It's how it's done. You don't...you can't do this.

[TALTHYBIUS]

Tell that to a man who hasn't lost his head.

[AJAX]
Seems more like he's lost his heart.

A noise within the tent. Both glance up and make a silent mutual agreement to change the subject, though Ajax's attempts at subtlety are clumsy at best.

So, did you hear who's coming into camp?

[TALTHYBIUS]
Who? Zeus and Hermes in disguise, looking for a hot meal and a roof above their heads?

[AJAX]
Could be. I was talking to the watchmen after dinner. They all swore up and down that they saw a wagon flying across the border, but no one could tell who was in it.

[TALTHYBIUS]
They're pulling your leg, kid.

[AJAX]
I don't know—

[TALTHYBIUS] *amused*
A *wagon*?

[AJAX]
They seemed pretty spooked to me.

[TALTHYBIUS]
Don't listen to a word they say. They like messing with you.

[AJAX]
No—

[TALTHYBIUS]
The three of you, you're the babies of the camp. You—

[AJAX]
We *were*, ten years ago.

Talthybius pauses.

[TALTHYBIUS]
Fair enough.

In the background, Iphis and Diomede react to something in great shock. They get Briseis' attention, and when she sees what they see, she, too, can barely restrain herself.

The sudden onset of hope does funny things to a man. I guess we're at the stage where we're all seeing things…

At that moment, Priam enters, his hair smeared with ashes and dirt. Talthybius sees him, but Ajax is oblivious.

[AJAX]
Maybe all our defectors have finally returned. Big surprise they'd pick a time like this. Things finally start looking up for us, and…

Ajax spots Priam, too. He and Talthybius stare in open shock. They are unsure whether to stand, to fight, to bow, to look away. Instead, they just go on staring.

[PRIAM]
Good evening, boys.

He moves slowly, painfully, but with dignity. He walks silently past them towards the tent.

[TALTHYBIUS / AJAX]
Your majesty…? / Hello, sir—

Priam slips past them into the tent and Ajax and Talthybius rise, but do not go after him.

Lights on the tent. Achilles and Priam regard each other.

[PRIAM]
Achilles.

Best of the Greeks. Aristos Achaion.

[ACHILLES]
Priam, King of Troy.

[PRIAM]
Hector's father.

Priam kneels.

I kiss the hands that killed my son.

[ACHILLES]
How did you get into the camp?

[PRIAM]
Does it matter?

[ACHILLES]
Who let you in?

[PRIAM]
Nobody.

[ACHILLES]
You shouldn't be here.

[PRIAM]
In my own kingdom?

[ACHILLES]
Get out.

[PRIAM]
Let me speak.

[ACHILLES]
Get out.

[PRIAM]
Let me speak, damn it—

[ACHILLES]

Get out. Get out or I won't spare your life.

[PRIAM]

You killed my son. What else can you do to me?

Both men are silent. Then, Priam places his hands on Achilles' knees, assuming the position of a suppliant. He says carefully, like a recitation:

All I ask, great Achilles, is that you think of your own father. He watches the sea, and he waits for you to return. He rejoices every time they bring news that you are still alive. He hopes, and he hopes, and he hopes. He thinks of the boy you were, the boy he raised—

[ACHILLES]

My father didn't raise me.

[PRIAM]

Then think of those who have been fathers to you. All of us are here because somebody loved us.

My city is in ruins. My family is torn apart. My Hector was all I had left. And now—well. By your grace, I would like to bring him home.

[ACHILLES]

Prepared words.

[PRIAM]

Would I have come all this way without them?

[ACHILLES]

What else have you prepared? I see that you brought ransom.

[PRIAM]

There's more in the chariot. Tripods, cloaks, robes, cauldrons. I have no more use for them. They will all be yours soon either way.

[ACHILLES]

If gifts were enough to win me over, you wouldn't be here in the first place.

[PRIAM]

You would rather rip them from our hands when our city burns?

[ACHILLES]

What use do I have for tripods, cloaks, robes, cauldrons?

[PRIAM]

What use do *I* have?

If I may make a suggestion, accept these gifts for your father. They are for your family to enjoy when you return home safe and sound. By Zeus, take them and let my boy go.

Achilles moves forward. Priam tenses, but Achilles is only drawing a chair.

[ACHILLES]

You should sit down.

[PRIAM]

Not while he lies here in filth.

[ACHILLES]

Don't. If you keep–I don't know what I might...

He collects himself with great effort. Finally, he says:

Sit. Please.

After a long moment, Priam sits, slowly. Achilles does, too. Achilles speaks after a silence, carefully conciliatory.

No man alive would have dared to do what you did today.

[PRIAM]

I know. My wife tried to stop me.

[ACHILLES]

Mmhm.

[PRIAM]

She begged me not to go, just as she begged Hector. I had to promise her I'd turn back at the first sign of trouble. I didn't.

[ACHILLES]

You didn't.

[PRIAM]

But to leave him here and let you drag him through the dirt—

[ACHILLES]

What should I have done? Bathe him? Honor him?

[PRIAM]

My son already died for what he did.

[ACHILLES]

And it wasn't good enough.

[PRIAM]

What else do you want?

[ACHILLES]

I want him back.

[PRIAM]

So do I.

[ACHILLES]

Your Majesty. I—Your son—he took everything from me, and
I—

[PRIAM]

Don't let him take your humanity.

*Both are tense as spooked animals, searching each other's faces for
signs of animosity. Perhaps this time, Achilles finds none.*

[ACHILLES]

How did you make it into our camp? Let alone our tent.

[PRIAM]

I suppose the gods were with me.

[ACHILLES]

Some gods. Look at the position we're both in.

[PRIAM]

Careful, young man. They are watching us tonight.

[ACHILLES]

What else can they do to us?

Neither man can respond. Achilles privately comes to a decision.

How many days would you need to
mourn and bury your son?

[PRIAM]

Even the timber for the pyre would be a long undertaking.
The hills are far, and our bravest men no longer dare to venture
outside the city walls.

He is carefully watching Achilles' face.

Nine days to mourn him. On the tenth, we will hold his funeral rites.

He checks Achilles' reaction. He is pushing.

On the eleventh, we will raise his burial mound. On the
twelfth, if we must, we will fight again.

[ACHILLES]
I wish we didn't have to.

[PRIAM]
So do I.

A moment of silence.

[ACHILLES]
I will hold back the army for eleven days.

[PRIAM]
What—what are you playing at?

[ACHILLES]
Your son deserves his honors.

[PRIAM]
Don't try your ruses on me. / Don't—

[ACHILLES]
/ This isn't a trick.

[PRIAM]
What reason do I have to trust you?

[ACHILLES]
What could I gain by deceiving you?

*By now, Priam is weeping, wanting more than anything to believe
him.*

[PRIAM]
Your gods will punish you for this, Achilles. Your gods will–

Achilles clasps Priam's hands

[ACHILLES]
Where are they?

At last, both men give in to grief. The emotional pitch of the moment seems almost a prelude to a vocal number. However, the music in both their lives has gone.

Outside, actors seal off the fourth wall of the tent. Achilles and Priam are now seen only in silhouette as they weep together. Somewhere in the camp, a soldier sits by the bonfire with his lyre and plays a mournful, hopeful song.

Other soldiers go about their duties and leisure: playing dice, sharpening swords, folding their mats after dinner, huddling together for late-night conversations. When anyone passes Achilles' tent, they pause for a moment, considering the extraordinary event happening within. Then, they go on their way, muttering a few words to each other before leaving well enough alone.

Back at the tent, Achilles invites Priam to break bread. Time passes. Their silhouettes fade. The ensemble mostly disperses, leaving behind empty firepits and gentle silence.

The lyre player leaves. The orchestra takes up his lullaby. Achilles takes down the tent wall, and he and Priam stand at the threshold.

[PRIAM]

Now that I've tasted food and drink again, I think I will be able
to sleep tonight.

[ACHILLES]

Stay.

If Agamemnon catches you, he might give you some trouble.
Spend the night here. I'll walk you to the border before the sun
rises.

Priam considers it. He truly does.

[PRIAM]

You may have spared my life, but I will not sleep among men
who would kill me.

*Both of them remember themselves, remember who they are to each
other.*

Be well, Prince Achilles.

*Achilles clasps his hands one more time. Then, he signals within the
tent. Iphis and Diomede exit with Hector's body, placing it in Priam's
chariot, with Briseis following behind.*

Right in front of Achilles, Briseis kneels and bows.

*And then Priam is gone. Achilles watches, ensuring his safe passage.
He does not leave the threshold of the tent.*

XVI

INTERLUDE II

Young Achilles and Young Patroclus go across the stage; they are still laughing, but this time, they are slower, stumbling out of breath.

At last, Achilles folds Patroclus' clothes and their blankets. He remembers something—he puts out bowls for the dogs—and then returns to his task.

Achilles unfolds the blankets, spreading them over the bed, and then folds them again.

[MIDDLE PATROCLUS] *off-stage*
Cold, cold, cold, cold—

Achilles looks. Middle Patroclus runs in, a wineskin across his back, soaking wet from head to toe. From the opposite side, Middle Achilles enters, folding a blanket of his own.

[MIDDLE ACHILLES]
Where were you?

[MIDDLE PATROCLUS]
What does it look like?

[MIDDLE ACHILLES]
What happened to—you went swimming without me?!

[MIDDLE PATROCLUS]
Cold.

Middle Patroclus shakes out his hair like a wet dog.

[MIDDLE ACHILLES]
Not on the blankets!

Middle Patroclus snatches up one of (adult) Achilles' just-folded blankets and wraps it around himself.

I just folded that, you menace.

[MIDDLE PATROCLUS]
The ocean is very, very cold.

[MIDDLE ACHILLES] *sarcastic*
Really?

[MIDDLE PATROCLUS] *serious*
So cold.

[MIDDLE ACHILLES]
Maybe if you hadn't gone first thing in
the morning, without / me—

[MIDDLE PATROCLUS]
/ I may be dying.

[MIDDLE ACHILLES]
That's your reward. You look like a drowned weasel.

[MIDDLE PATROCLUS]
No, I don't.

[MIDDLE ACHILLES]
Yes, you do.

Middle Achilles wraps his own blanket around Middle Patroclus, draping it over his head so that his ears are sticking out.

Yes, you do.

A bout of play-fighting.

By now, lights have partially faded on Achilles, such that only his silhouette is present in the scene. The two prepare for breakfast, and Middle Achilles takes note of the wineskin.

Wine before breakfast?

[MIDDLE PATROCLUS] *with a secret smile*
Oh, just water.

[MIDDLE ACHILLES]
That explains why you aren't complaining about a headache.

You seem happy this morning.

[MIDDLE PATROCLUS]
Well.

His smile grows wider, and Middle Achilles is perplexed and delighted—and a little apprehensive.

[MIDDLE ACHILLES]
You're smiling.

[MIDDLE PATROCLUS]
Does Prince Achilles forbid me to smile?

[MIDDLE ACHILLES]
Can I guess what you're thinking?

[MIDDLE PATROCLUS]
No, you can't.

Middle Achilles assesses Middle Patroclus' happy mood with suspicion, then picks up the wineskin and inspects it.

[MIDDLE ACHILLES] *joking*
You swear it's just water in here?

Middle Patroclus surprise attacks Middle Achilles and pulls the wineskin away from him.

Middle Patroclus looks over at Middle Achilles' plate.

[MIDDLE PATROCLUS]
Don't you want more of that?

[MIDDLE ACHILLES]
I should be quick. / Actually—

[MIDDLE PATROCLUS]
/ Low tide isn't 'til noon. There'll be plenty of time for us to get to the / cove.

[MIDDLE ACHILLES] *apologetic*
/ No, I have to meet with the officers.

[MIDDLE PATROCLUS]
What for?

[MIDDLE ACHILLES] *proud*
Turns out the big ship won't be seaworthy by tomorrow. Odysseus tasked me with crew reassignments.

[MIDDLE PATROCLUS]
Do you need any help?

[MIDDLE ACHILLES]
Odysseus will be there. He and I should have it covered.

[MIDDLE PATROCLUS]
I'll wait here, then. We can go up to the cove when you get back.

Finish up the fish sauce, at least. We can't take it with us tomorrow.

[MIDDLE ACHILLES]
I'm not that hungry. I actually ate over at the palace.

[MIDDLE PATROCLUS]
Right. How was your son?

[MIDDLE ACHILLES]
Small. Red.

[MIDDLE PATROCLUS]
Loud?

[MIDDLE ACHILLES]
He was only fussy because I woke him up.

[MIDDLE PATROCLUS]
I can't blame him.

[MIDDLE ACHILLES]
The princess says he's like that around everyone.

[MIDDLE PATROCLUS]
He's two.

[MIDDLE ACHILLES]
One and a half. But he's so smart already. He grabbed Odysseus' cloak and said, "Purple." / Purple!

[MIDDLE PATROCLUS]
/ He knows his colors already?

[MIDDLE ACHILLES]
At least that one. I'll go see him one more time tonight. Maybe he'll like me better if I bring him something to play with.

[MIDDLE PATROCLUS]
Maybe one of those spinning tops? The ones / that—

[MIDDLE ACHILLES]
/ Would he know what to do with it?

[MIDDLE PATROCLUS]
You could spin it for him. He might enjoy watching.

[MIDDLE ACHILLES]
He's a prince. He's got everything already. I don't know what else I can give him.

[MIDDLE PATROCLUS]
That won't matter. It'll be from you.

[MIDDLE ACHILLES]
Pass me those olives.

[MIDDLE PATROCLUS]
Now you're hungry.

[MIDDLE ACHILLES]
Olives.

[MIDDLE PATROCLUS]
Not a chance. I'm stuffing them.

[MIDDLE ACHILLES]
And you're going to keep them to yourself?

[MIDDLE PATROCLUS]
They're for our trip to the cove.

[MIDDLE ACHILLES]
Right.

[MIDDLE PATROCLUS]
It's a long walk to the other side of the island. You know you'll
start complaining.

[MIDDLE ACHILLES]
Actually, Patroclus.

[MIDDLE PATROCLUS]
What?

[MIDDLE ACHILLES]
There's, there might also be—

The princess warned me there might be a surprise celebration
for us. Before we leave for Troy tomorrow.

A beat.

[MIDDLE PATROCLUS]
That explains a lot.

[MIDDLE ACHILLES]
Does it?

[MIDDLE PATROCLUS]
I caught the girls practicing some kind of dance yesterday.
They ran when they saw me.

[MIDDLE ACHILLES]
Girls always run when they—

Middle Patroclus attacks him before he can finish that insult.

We'll still go up to the cove. When the celebration is over.

[MIDDLE PATROCLUS]
Your son.

[MIDDLE ACHILLES]
After.

[MIDDLE PATROCLUS]
We'll miss the tidepools. It'll be well past low tide.

[MIDDLE ACHILLES]
Right.

[MIDDLE PATROCLUS]
There'll be beaches at Troy.

Should we be eating breakfast, then? Do you think they'll feed us?

[MIDDLE ACHILLES]
It'll be a lousy surprise if they don't.

[MIDDLE PATROCLUS]
And poor manners. It'll be our last good meal for a while.

[MIDDLE ACHILLES]
I'll miss those little Skyrian cheeses.

[MIDDLE PATROCLUS]
The round ones.

[MIDDLE ACHILLES]
Maybe we can take some with us.

[MIDDLE PATROCLUS]
Ask them if we can have those instead of the gifts.

[MIDDLE ACHILLES]
Brilliant.

[MIDDLE PATROCLUS]
There'll be plenty of arrowheads at Troy. Not nearly enough cheese.

[MIDDLE ACHILLES]
You should have been a diplomat, not a soldier.

[MIDDLE PATROCLUS]
Make sure to ask for honey to go with them.

[MIDDLE ACHILLES]
You drive a tough bargain.

[MIDDLE PATROCLUS]
Go ahead and eat the olives. We need to finish them, anyway.

[MIDDLE ACHILLES]
We could go to the cliffs one more time tonight.

[MIDDLE PATROCLUS]
You know what Odysseus said. Up before dawn tomorrow—

[MIDDLE ACHILLES]
—or the song is sung without us.

[MIDDLE PATROCLUS]
Why does he talk like that?

[MIDDLE ACHILLES]
He's the first king I've met who talks like a king.

[MIDDLE PATROCLUS]
He's just a prince.

[MIDDLE ACHILLES] *enthusiastic*
He may as well be a king.

[MIDDLE PATROCLUS] *sarcastic*
He acts like one.

[MIDDLE ACHILLES] *enthusiastic*
He does. It's like—the bards tell the stories, and the stories always have kings in them. So the kings are always well-spoken. I thought they were all supposed to sound like that. I didn't know what I'd do when I took the throne.

The unspoken hangs in the air. Perhaps Middle Achilles hadn't meant to say that. Finally, an affectionate gesture from Middle Patroclus to Middle Achilles.

[MIDDLE PATROCLUS]
I wouldn't want a storyteller for a king.

A beat. Something is unaddressed, unresolved.

[MIDDLE ACHILLES]
/ Patroclus,

[MIDDLE PATROCLUS]
/ You should go meet with Odysseus, Achilles. You shouldn't be late.

[MIDDLE ACHILLES]
Walk with me there.

[MIDDLE PATROCLUS]
I'll start packing. Come get me for the celebration.

[MIDDLE ACHILLES]
Don't tell the princess I spoiled the surprise. She'll never forgive me.

[MIDDLE PATROCLUS]
She already won't forgive you for leaving again.

[MIDDLE ACHILLES]
So I can't spoil her surprise, too.

A beat.

[MIDDLE PATROCLUS]
I really hope there'll be a feast.

[MIDDLE ACHILLES]
Me too.

[MIDDLE PATROCLUS]
Good wine—

[MIDDLE ACHILLES & MIDDLE PATROCLUS]
And a good roast.

[MIDDLE PATROCLUS]
It'll be a good time.

Silence. They can't quite meet each other's eyes.

[MIDDLE ACHILLES]
I thought you might be angry with me.

[MIDDLE PATROCLUS]
About what?

[MIDDLE ACHILLES]
Are you?

[MIDDLE PATROCLUS]
You weren't the one who planned the meeting.

[MIDDLE ACHILLES]
Not—

[MIDDLE PATROCLUS]
Or the celebration.

[MIDDLE ACHILLES]
Not that.

I've had this conversation in my head a hundred times, Patroclus. But we leave for Troy tomorrow, and you haven't said a word.

[MIDDLE PATROCLUS]
Should I have?

[MIDDLE ACHILLES]
If there's anything you want to say.

[MIDDLE PATROCLUS]
If I said I didn't want you to go to Troy, would it change your mind?

A beat.

[MIDDLE ACHILLES]
I'd want to know.

[MIDDLE PATROCLUS]
Now you do. And so do I.

A beat. A beat.

[MIDDLE ACHILLES]
Let's go.

[MIDDLE PATROCLUS]
You go. I'll come later.

[MIDDLE ACHILLES]
Not there.

The beginnings of hope.

[MIDDLE PATROCLUS]
Where?

[MIDDLE ACHILLES]
Wherever.

We can't go far. I'll have to be back for—

[MIDDLE PATROCLUS] *back to reality*
I know.

[MIDDLE ACHILLES]
Just to the trees on the hill?

[MIDDLE PATROCLUS]
I hate that walk.

[MIDDLE ACHILLES]
Why?

[MIDDLE PATROCLUS]
Rocks in my shoes.

[MIDDLE ACHILLES] *imitating him*
"Rocks in my shoes."

[MIDDLE PATROCLUS] *starting to smile*
My olives.

[MIDDLE ACHILLES]
We'll take them with us, you prodigy.

Middle Patroclus is giggling now.

Well, Patroclus?

[MIDDLE PATROCLUS]
Well, what?

[MIDDLE ACHILLES]
How do you want to spend the next few moments?

[ACHILLES & MIDDLE PATROCLUS]
With you.

[MIDDLE ACHILLES]
You've been doing that for the last ten years.

Lights fade on Middle Achilles and Patroclus. Sole focus is now on the lone figure of Achilles.

[ACHILLES]
I always wanted it, Patroclus. Everything we had. But you were always so good at knowing what you wanted. I was only good at wanting. I woke up one day and there were all these things I didn't know. And I started wanting them, too, because I wouldn't have known what to do with myself if I didn't. But I always wanted you. That never changed.

Patroclus enters. He isn't wearing the bloodied shirt that he wore in "Visitations." He looks very much like the Patroclus we knew from Act I.

[PATROCLUS]
Did you save any dinner for me?

[ACHILLES]
Stop it.

[PATROCLUS]
I was just asking.

Achilles laughs weakly. When Patroclus joins in, the laugh becomes full and helpless.

[ACHILLES] *still laughing*
How did this happen?

[PATROCLUS]
Well.

[ACHILLES]
We were never supposed to be without each other.

[PATROCLUS]
Not if I had any say in it.

[ACHILLES]
You did. Isn't that the reason we're...

[PATROCLUS]
Unfair.

[ACHILLES]
Unwise.

[ACHILLES / PATROCLUS]
Unwise and unnecessary. / Unsound and unnecessary.

[ACHILLES]
Unsound. Unsound and unnecessary.

[PATROCLUS]
Remember what you once said about growing up? How it's
like—

[ACHILLES & PATROCLUS]
Running after someone,

[PATROCLUS]
but always falling behind?

[ACHILLES]
Yes.

[PATROCLUS]
I felt like that sometimes when we were boys. You were King Peleus' golden son; I was a disgraced prince in exile.

I felt like that again when you refused to fight. You were always running just ahead of me, and there I was, afraid to touch you, like you'd slip away the moment I did.

[ACHILLES]
I left your cut on the table.

[PATROCLUS]
What?

[ACHILLES]
The pork. The last of mine.

[PATROCLUS]
Oh.

[ACHILLES]
Look, Patroclus. Centaurus is rising.

Patroclus rests his head on Achilles' shoulder. They are sitting side by side; they are children reckoning with a world they can't understand.

[PATROCLUS]

I see him.

[ACHILLES]

Maybe—maybe someone will tell our story, just like they told
Cleopatra and Meleager's. Look at our stars
and see constellations.

[PATROCLUS]

Maybe they will.

[ACHILLES]

Do you think so, Patroclus?

[PATROCLUS]

Yes. Yes, they will. But I don't want them to.

[ACHILLES]

Why?

[PATROCLUS]

They'll say it was a sad story.

The sound of laughter. Lights fade back in on Middle Achilles and Patroclus. They are sitting on a blanket with their bounty, reclining like young gods. Off the end of Achilles' line, they began laughing hard over something, trying not to upset their plates or spit out their food.

[MIDDLE ACHILLES]

But Odysseus' face, it looked like—you know? The face he does? Like he's just heard the sorriest story in the world, but he's also trying not to laugh at it. So the princess went out and she—

He looks up to see Middle Patroclus reaching for the wineskin and notes his mischievous look with suspicion.

You're still smiling. / What is going on with—

[MIDDLE PATROCLUS]

/ No, I'm not.

[MIDDLE ACHILLES]

Wait, is this like the time you said you weren't / going to—

Middle Patroclus settles innocently, the wineskin in his lap.

[MIDDLE PATROCLUS]

/ Well, I wasn't *lying*—

[MIDDLE ACHILLES]

You knew.

[MIDDLE PATROCLUS]

No, I didn't.

[MIDDLE ACHILLES]

Yes, you / did!

[MIDDLE PATROCLUS]
/ Your bowl!

Middle Patroclus lunges to right Middle Achilles' bowl—and nearly knocks a few things over in the process. Both break into renewed laughter.

[MIDDLE ACHILLES]
You will destroy this whole island.

[MIDDLE PATROCLUS]
And whose fault will that be?

[MIDDLE ACHILLES]
Yours. Just like the time / that—

[MIDDLE PATROCLUS]
/ That was seven years / ago.

[MIDDLE ACHILLES]
/ Six. Wasn't that the summer that we went / back to the—

[MIDDLE PATROCLUS]
/ No?

[MIDDLE ACHILLES]
Because that was when / we—

[MIDDLE PATROCLUS]
/ When the—

[MIDDLE ACHILLES]
Right.

[MIDDLE PATROCLUS]
I forgot about that.

[MIDDLE ACHILLES]
Me too.

[MIDDLE PATROCLUS]
Sorry. You were telling me—

[MIDDLE ACHILLES]
Right.

No, that was after—

[MIDDLE PATROCLUS]
Odysseus.

[MIDDLE ACHILLES]
Right. Anyway, anyway, Odysseus came back, and the princess
went out to the beach to look.

Middle Patroclus rises again.

I thought I should go with her. The stench was so awful. I
thought there might be a body or something. And I said that, but
it only encouraged her. I think—personally, I think she liked the
idea of—but mixed with all that seawater, it smelled like something / out of—

Middle Patroclus is approaching Middle Achilles from behind, wine-skin in hand.

[MIDDLE PATROCLUS]
/ Funny that you'd mention seawater.

[MIDDLE ACHILLES]
Wha—

As Middle Achilles turns back to look at him, Middle Patroclus dumps the entire wineskin full of seawater over Middle Achilles' head.

You—

[MIDDLE PATROCLUS / MIDDLE ACHILLES] *ad lib*
You wanted to go for a swim— / I should've known you were up to something—
You wanted me to take you— / You won't get away with this—
I only brought the ocean to you— / You will never forget this day—

Middle Patroclus begins running before Middle Achilles even springs to his feet. The chase that ensues is short, and it ends with Middle Achilles wrestling the wineskin from Middle Patroclus' hands and dumping the remaining contents over his head. The two are tumbling to the ground together, soaking wet, laughing and laughing.

[MIDDLE ACHILLES] *pulling seaweed out of his hair*
There was seaweed in there!

[MIDDLE PATROCLUS]
It's the ocean. What did you expect?

*Middle Achilles tries to throw the seaweed at Middle Patroclus. It's
seaweed. It doesn't go well.*

[MIDDLE ACHILLES]
I hate you.

[MIDDLE PATROCLUS]
No.

[ACHILLES]
Let me see. What happened after that?

*Middle Patroclus stands and reaches down to help Middle Achilles
up. Lights begin to fade on their pocket of the stage.*

*Patroclus stands over Achilles, but they are no longer sharing the
same light. By the moment, Patroclus' spotlight grows colder and colder.*

After the meal, Odysseus was talking with Ajax about it all,
and one of the messengers—what's his name? You knew him, Patroclus, you talked with him all the time—

[PATROCLUS]
You know what the worst part is, Achilles?

[ACHILLES]
What?

[PATROCLUS]

Promise not to hate me for it.

[ACHILLES]

I'll do my best.

[PATROCLUS]

I'm glad we went together.

Lights fade on Patroclus. Achilles is alone.

As Achilles is speaking, Middle Patroclus walks by him and puts his blanket around Achilles' shoulders. Then, he, too, slips quietly away and exits.

[ACHILLES]

It isn't really that funny, actually. You would've laughed. Even though you shouldn't have. The messenger came through the doorway, and he gave us a single look, but Odysseus sprang to his feet. And Ajax fell back, like that, he wasn't expecting it. And it also was beginning to smell like smoke...

Achilles is alone, continuing to talk to Patroclus in the emptiness as lights fade.

XVII

NOSTOS

*J*ust *before dawn in the camp. Achilles approaches Odysseus' tent, from which an actor rolls back the fourth wall.*

Odysseus is in a chair, perhaps puzzling over a petteia board, perhaps carving a small wooden figure. Achilles stands outside with his lyre. He does not go in.

[ODYSSEUS] *barely looking up*
Yes, unfortunately, I am awake. Come in.

Achilles does. Odysseus looks up in surprise.

Prince Achilles.

[ACHILLES]
Odysseus.

He is wary, defensive, and tense, a hunted animal easily spooked.

[ODYSSEUS]
Here to drive the sun chariot?

[ACHILLES]
I've come to ask a favor.

[ODYSSEUS]
That isn't something I ever expected to hear.

[ACHILLES]
Do you think I wanted to look for you?

His tone is barely angry, mostly exhausted.

[ODYSSEUS]
Peace. Tell me what you've come here to say.

Achilles nearly turns back. The words do not come easy, but rise haltingly above his wounded pride.

[ACHILLES]
I saw him. He visited me in a dream. He asked me to give him his rites and burn his body.

[ODYSSEUS]
Hector?

[ACHILLES]
I've taken care of him.

He looked exactly like he used to. His eyes. He asked me to mix our ashes together in the same urn, just like we grew up on Mount Pelion side by side.

[ODYSSEUS]

Well, when a dead man supplicates, how can you deny him?

[ACHILLES]

You don't believe me?

[ODYSSEUS]

I never said that.

[ACHILLES]

I will respect his wishes. Today, I will hold his funeral.

[ODYSSEUS]

We can certainly see to that.

[ACHILLES]

That's not what I'm asking of you.

I won't live long, now that Hector is dead. Afterwards, my ashes. Would you ensure...?

[ODYSSEUS]

If you don't mind me asking, why me?

Achilles gazes at the embroidered cloak that is draped over the chair. Odysseus looks, too. Odysseus does not respond, but all is understood.

[ACHILLES]

You would want someone to do the same for you.

When Odysseus speaks again, his tone is gentler.

[ODYSSEUS]

So what will these magnificent funeral rites entail?

[ACHILLES]

Chariot racing. Archery. Sparring. Only the best for Patroclus.

[ODYSSEUS]

Naturally.

[ACHILLES]

And sacrifices at the funeral pyre, of course.

[ODYSSEUS]

Sheep, cattle, goats...?

[ACHILLES]

As many livestock as we can muster.

[ODYSSEUS]

We do need to eat, you know.

[ACHILLES]

The war will be over soon.

[ODYSSEUS]

Fair enough. I will fetch men to prepare the rites.

[ACHILLES]
No need. I have seen to it.

[ODYSSEUS]
Well, it looks like you've thought of everything.

[ACHILLES]
This lyre was my mother's. When you sail past Skyros on your way home, give it to my son.

[ODYSSEUS] *news to him*
Your son?

[ACHILLES]
Pyrrhus.

I only met him once. Maybe he doesn't play.

[ODYSSEUS]
How old…?

[ACHILLES]
Almost twelve now. I was taking shelter on Skyros, after word got out about the prophecies. I was someone else. It was the freest time of my life. But.

[ODYSSEUS]
Yes.

[ACHILLES]
I got to meet him when we docked there

on the way to Troy. He was a troublemaker.

[ODYSSEUS]
I'm surprised.

Almost an exchanged smile.

[ACHILLES]
Also.

Achilles touches his own hair.

I swore a vow to my mother. I kept this lock of hair to sacrifice it to the gods in thanks when I...when I return home.

I would like to burn it on Patroclus' pyre today.

[ODYSSEUS]
It's a lovely gesture. I'll make sure you have the chance.

A beat. Achilles says nothing further. A beat.

When you fought yesterday, you took blow after blow, barely rising to defend yourself. We all tried to intervene, but could not break through the ranks. At the deciding moment, one of the soldiers had you on the ground and nearly made an end of it. But then I noticed you curled up. Too quickly to be a conscious thought. Rolled over to shield your face.

[ACHILLES] *defensive*
What are you trying to say?

[ODYSSEUS]
Are you still afraid?

Here. Let me.

Odysseus moves his things from his chair, and Achilles regards him for a long moment. Finally, he goes, seats himself. Odysseus deftly begins to braid the lock of hair.

My son has terribly unruly hair. Just like his mother. Born with a full head of it. Like a wild mountain boy, his nurse said. Even when he was an infant, I had to cut it right against the skull so it wouldn't mat. His mother and I came up with the cleverest stratagems just to make him hold still.

Odysseus sings softly, almost to himself, as he finishes braiding Achilles' hair.

TOMORROW PERHAPS I WILL MEET WITH THE GODS'
NIGHT BEFORE I'VE RETURNED TO HER SIDE
MY ONE CONSOLATION IS WHEN I AWAKEN I KNOW
THAT I'LL SEE HER IN TIME

FOR WHERE SHE GOES
I WILL GO WITH HER

He cuts off the lock of hair.

There. For Patroclus.

Odysseus puts it in Achilles' hands, and Achilles looks at it for a long moment.

Well?

[ACHILLES]
I suppose I'll head back now.

[ODYSSEUS]
A wise decision. You have a big day ahead of you.

Achilles begins to head towards the doorway, then stops short.

[ACHILLES]
I was wondering.

[ODYSSEUS]
At your service.

[ACHILLES]
Did Patroclus speak with you the night before he fought?

[ODYSSEUS] *on guard*
He did.

[ACHILLES]
What did he say to you?

Odysseus is more unsettled than we have ever seen him.

[ODYSSEUS]
Achilles, I—Patroclus…

When he came to speak with me, he was already resolved to convince you somehow to fight, but he—

[ACHILLES]
I mean—do you know if he…? When he made his plan, did he know that he would…?

Odysseus understands Achilles' question now. He collects himself.

[ODYSSEUS]
He never meant to die for you.

Achilles' relief is so deep that it appears more like grief. He accepts Odysseus' answer.

[ACHILLES]
You will be there today?

[ODYSSEUS]
Wouldn't miss it for the world.

[ACHILLES]
We won't start the funeral games until after sunrise. You should get some rest.

[ODYSSEUS]
I won't.

[ACHILLES]
You won't.

Achilles exits.

XVIII

FUNERAL PYRES

*M*usic. The Greeks, led by Achilles, place Patroclus' body on a pyre. Achilles closes Patroclus' fingers around the lock of hair. A quiet farewell. The men crowd around the pyre as Phoenix sets it alight.

In the distance, another fire rises. On both sides of the border, a hero burns.

Time passes; the music dwindles down. The soldiers stand around the dying fire, almost expectant for something to happen. This cannot be how it ends: smoke and ash and silence.

But they leave one by one as the fire dies. When it is well and truly over, Briseis steps forward to collect the ashes. Achilles stops her and does it himself.

On the opposite side of the stage, Priam stands amidst his ruined kingdom, gazing into the distance, watching the light of Patroclus' funeral pyre dwindle down to nothing.

Achilles gives the urn to Odysseus. The sense of a torch passed.

All exit except Achilles.

XIX

THE RIVER

*A*chilles is alone in a single spotlight. He tunes his lyre, plucks a few stray tunes. It's unsettlingly intimate. Perhaps he is, at last, confronting his mortality. Perhaps he is dead already. Perhaps he is outside the world of the story—and in the theater with us.

[ACHILLES]
THE AFTERNOON WAS YELLOW
AND THE SUN WAS IN HIS HAIR
AND NOBODY WAS THERE BUT HIM AND I
WE SAT BESIDE THE RIVER
AND WE THREW OUR PEBBLES FAR
LAUGHING 'BOUT THE WAYS THAT WE MIGHT DIE

SHE NAMED ME ACHILLEUS—
"SORROW OF THE PEOPLE"
SHE TOLD ME THAT THIS WAS MY STRENGTH
IN YOUR DARKEST HOUR, YOU WOULD NEED A HERO
AND SO YOU SEE THE MAN THAT I BECAME

HE FOUND ANOTHER PEBBLE

AND HE PUT IT IN MY HAND
PULLING ME TO STAND AND THROW IT HIGH
IT FELL INTO THE WATER
AND WE WATCHED IT DISAPPEAR
AND HE SAW THAT THERE WAS
TEARSHINE IN MY EYES

SHE NAMED ME ACHILLEUS—
"SORROW OF THE PEOPLE"
YOU SAID I LIVED UP TO MY NAME
ALWAYS OVERFLOWING, FEELING FAR TOO FREELY
BUT YOU TOLD ME I COULD STAND TO FEEL SOME
SHAME

ACHILLEUS
ACHILLEUS
"SWIFT-FOOTED," "LION-HEARTED," "PELEUS' SON"
I SAW THE GIFT SHE GAVE ME TURN TO POISON ON
YOUR TONGUE
AND I KNEW IT WAS TOO LATE TO RUN

YOU SAID THAT I'D GET OLDER
AND ONE DAY I'D GET WISER
WHEN I TRIED TO SHOW YOU MY PAIN
DON'T YOU KNOW YOU PROMISED I'LL STAY YOUNG
FOREVER
IF THIS IS THE LIFE THAT I CLAIM?

ACHILLEUS
ACHILLEUS
"SWIFT-FOOTED," "LION-HEARTED," "PELEUS' SON"

IN TIME, I DIDN'T RECOGNIZE
MY NAME UPON HIS LIPS
'CAUSE WHATEVER YOU'D CALL ME, I'D COME

MY OLD DREAM RETURNS TO HAUNT ME
WHERE THEY'RE LAUGHING AS I'M DROWNING
AND I SLEEP BY HIS SIDE BUT I DREAM THAT HE HAS
FOUND ME
BUT THE TIDE TURNS SO DARK
WHEN I GLANCE IN HIS EYES
SO I STRIKE FOR HIS HEART
BUT I CAN'T GET A LIGHT
AND I SWORE.
I SWORE I WOULD GO WHERE HE GOES
BUT WHAT HAVE I COME TO? HEAVEN ONLY KNOWS
TELL THEM ALL WHY I DID IT. BUT CONFESS WHAT
YOU'VE DONE
WHEN THEY ASK WHY YOU DID IT, YOU'LL JUST SAY
THAT YOU WON

I WAKE UP IN THE MORNING WITH A RIVER
THROUGH MY CHEST
AND NOTHING TO PROTECT EXCEPT MY PRIDE
AND IF YOU REACHED INSIDE YOU'D FIND MY HEART
HAS TURNED TO STONE
BUT YOU NEED ME AT YOUR SIDE AND I MUST RISE

Lights fade.

ACT III:
BRISEIS

XX

POLYTROPOS

The sound comes first. Then, the lights. It is afternoon. At a distance, soldiers mill around the camp. They clean cauldrons, sharpen weapons, engage in practice bouts, all of this noise weaving into a cheerful percussive rhythm. A little ways away, Iphis and Diomede sort through baskets of laundry, singing a folk tune in a rhythm all its own.

Briseis is conferring with Talthybius by a tent. She presses a small sack into Talthybius' hands.

[BRISEIS]

Hector is dead. Achilles is dead. It's over. You know what will become of us when Troy falls. Think about your mother, your sister, your girl.

[TALTHYBIUS]

What's this for?

[BRISEIS]

This is all I have left to give you. Give me audience with Odysseus. Make any excuse.

[TALTHYBIUS]
Letting you sneak around to see your friends is one thing, but
Odysseus...

Briseis produces another sack from the folds of her garment.

[BRISEIS]
Then name your price.

[TALTHYBIUS]
Where did you even...

Iphis and Diomede pick up their baskets.

[IPHIS] *calling*
Are you ready to go, Briseis?

[BRISEIS]
Go without me, Iphis. I'll catch up.

*Talthybius hesitates another moment, and then leads Briseis offstage.
She walks with unflinching poise, but her hands fidget—which doesn't
escape Iphis and Diomede's notice.*

The two walk together, carrying the laundry.

[IPHIS]
She keeps going off alone.

[DIOMEDE]
She's always been like that.

[IPHIS]

But something is different, Diomede. I don't know.

[DIOMEDE]

She fidgets with her hands. She never used to do that.

[IPHIS]

I think it's a game she used to have with Patroclus. He made
shadow figures so she could follow the stories the Greeks were
telling.

Iphis makes a bird with her hands.

[DIOMEDE]

Rain? Oh, bird.

[DIOMEDE]

Seabird. That's her favorite.

*Diomede tries it out with her own hands. The two make a brief
game out of attempting other shapes. Then, Diomede glances back to
make sure they will not be overheard.*

I wonder how they'll tell this one. At the end of the day, that's
all it took. Just—

She mimes the flight of an arrow.

[IPHIS]

Can you imagine? The epic tale of Achilles, felled by an arrow
in the thick of battle like any common soldier.

[DIOMEDE]

Serves him right.

What? You don't think so?

[IPHIS]

Why wouldn't I? It's just…we would've been lucky to go back to Mount Pelion after the war, wouldn't we?

[DIOMEDE]

They were never going back to "Mount Pelion," Iphis. If that's even a real place. And they all say Achilles' mother was a goddess. If that were really true, why are they both dust?

[IPHIS]

What? Would it have been better to go to Odysseus or Ajax?

[DIOMEDE]

If I let myself think about could-have-beens—

[IPHIS]

Or would you have preferred to go to Agamemnon?

[DIOMEDE]

You know he already has his sights set on Briseis.

[IPHIS]

When have men ever stopped at enough?

Behind them, an actor lifts the fourth wall of Odysseus' tent. Talthybius is leading Briseis inside with heaps of riches; Odysseus and Talthybius are having a silent conversation.

[DIOMEDE]
Day after tomorrow, we'll know exactly where we're going.

[IPHIS]
You have bets on which of them will win Achilles' funeral games?

[DIOMEDE]
You know who it'll be. It'll be

[IPHIS & DIOMEDE] *with scorn*
Aristos Achaion.

[DIOMEDE]
The best of the Greeks.

[IPHIS]
The prince of the dogs.

[DIOMEDE]
The god of the fleas.

Iphis and Diomede exit. Talthybius exits, too, not without an uneasy backwards glance.

[ODYSSEUS]
I assume you aren't here to show me

what I stand to win at the funeral games.

[BRISEIS]
No, sir.

[ODYSSEUS]
Good. I'm not much wanting for gold, and I'm not looking to
forget my wife, either.

[BRISEIS]
I'm happy to hear that, sir.

[ODYSSEUS]
Well. Out with it.

[BRISEIS]
Patroclus spoke with you the night before the Trojans stormed
the camp.

[ODYSSEUS]
I'd left my cloak in his tent. He was always thoughtful.

[BRISEIS]
He looked for you the next day, too. Everyone thought that
would be the day of Trojan victory, but he still said your people
would prevail.

[ODYSSEUS]
Hope springs eternal.

[BRISEIS]

And he tried to say goodbye to me.

It was you who put Patroclus in Achilles' armor that day.

A beat.

[ODYSSEUS]

He did come to me. The night before. He was determined to find any way to save his people—and save Achilles from disgrace. The idea was his. I only refined the details.

[BRISEIS]

You want to go home, sir. You will do whatever it takes to return.

[ODYSSEUS]

Yes.

[BRISEIS]

It ended both their lives.

[ODYSSEUS]

I know you cared for Patroclus. I don't expect you would understand. A man would do anything for the smallest chance of seeing his home again.

[BRISEIS]

I understand better than you do, sir.

I will keep your secret.

[ODYSSEUS]
If you told, who would believe you?

[BRISEIS]
If anyone did, he would admire you all the more. But they don't need to believe me. I don't mean to wound your name.

I wondered why you wouldn't put your name on the plan that turned the war around. I thought it might be part of a greater scheme, but nothing further happened to explain it.

[ODYSSEUS]
So what was your conclusion?

[BRISEIS]
You are sorry. You want your part in it forgotten. It will never be as long as I'm around.

[ODYSSEUS]
I could kill you.

[BRISEIS]
Yes, sir. If you don't help me, that will be a mercy. But your hands will show the blood of both of us who loved Achilles.

Odysseus' tone assumes its old wry confidence; he believes he has re-gained the upper hand.

[ODYSSEUS]
You weave a clever tale, girl.

[BRISEIS]

I don't mean to be "clever," sir.

[ODYSSEUS]

We all know it was Patroclus who you loved.

[BRISEIS]

Is that what you believe of me?

Then would you rather your hands show the blood of both of
us who loved Patroclus?

[ODYSSEUS]

What do you need from me, Briseis?

[BRISEIS]

I understand that you are sailing to Skyros
to recruit Achilles' son.

[ODYSSEUS]

It's what Agamemnon asked of me.

[BRISEIS]

Bring us aboard your ship as slaves. Me, Iphis, and Diomede.
At Skyros, you will offer us as a gift of friendship to the king, one
of many gifts in exchange for the boy. I have heard of the king's
kindness and hospitality. We will live among his daughters, just
as Achilles did.

[ODYSSEUS]

What if I decide not to sail to Skyros after all?

[BRISEIS]

In this life, I have become the lowest of the low. But I believe I am fortunate to be so small a person. My life follows no prophecies. The gods have forgotten me. No fate is final. I can always hope.

XXI

INTERLUDE III / IPHIGENIA

*T*he ensemble softly suggests the crackle of bonfires, the campwide
murmur of late evening.

*Achilles and Patroclus are sitting by their tent; Achilles is playing his
lyre. Over a simple acoustic guitar rendition of "Where You Go,"
Odysseus, Ajax, and Phoenix enter. For an instant, the walls of time collapse, and it is as if we have returned to the start of the show: the embassy to Achilles and the beginning of the end. While in Act I, Odysseus
had seemed cool and unruffled, this time, we see him as he truly was:
pausing and lingering, witnessing the quiet moment between the pair,
standing apart from the rest.*

*Ajax and Phoenix move forward and prepare the stage for the next
scene. It is clear that they do not see Achilles and Patroclus there.
Odysseus, however, simply stands there. When Ajax glances back and
motions Odysseus along, the illusion is broken, and Achilles and Patroclus exit. Achilles hands his lyre to Odysseus on his way out. We are back
in the present moment.*

Odysseus, Ajax, and Phoenix settle down around a fire. Odysseus takes up his instrument and begins to play.

[ODYSSEUS]
SO SHE WENT TO HIM
IN THE FATEFUL DARK
AS THE ASHES FELL LIKE STARS

AND HER TEARS WERE BIRDS
AND THEY TRAVELED FAR
AND THEY NESTED IN HIS HEART

AND SHE SAYS HIS NAME
AND IT FELL LIKE ARROWS
THAT THUNDER FROM THE SKY

EVERY SYLLABLE
WAS A BATTLE CRY—
AND SHE HELD HIM AS HE DIED—

Odysseus seems put out by his own song. He tunes his lyre as Agamemnon enters and takes a seat.

[AGAMEMNON]
An invigoratingly cheerful tune.

[ODYSSEUS]
Glad you think so.

[AJAX]
What's gotten into you?

[ODYSSEUS]

You know me. Old and melancholy.

[AJAX]

You're not old.

[ODYSSEUS]

Will be by the time I get home.

[AGAMEMNON]

If you'd brought us Achilles' son, we might've been through here already.

[ODYSSEUS]

We won't discuss this in front of Phoenix.

[AJAX]

Odysseus, I do believe he's asleep.

Phoenix snores in confirmation. Ajax goes to find a blanket and pulls it over him.

[ODYSSEUS]

The war is on the verge of being won. Forgive my lack of modesty, but I'd say my tactical gifts are needed here more than ever.

[AGAMEMNON]

Those tactical gifts are exactly what we need to coax Pyrrhus out of his mother's arms. Why do you think I'm sending you?

We've got good soldiers, Odysseus, but they're exhausted. We haven't managed to take the city on our own. Even with Hector out of the way. They need a champion to inspire them to victory. I've got no delusions. That isn't you, that isn't you, and it sure as hell isn't me.

I'm not asking for golden apples. Just sail to Skyros, get the boy, and bring him back here.

[ODYSSEUS]

If I may speak plainly, sir, I'd prefer that someone else be sent.

[AGAMEMNON]

What? In the tenth year of the war, after sending countless men to their personal dooms, is the great Odysseus experiencing a twinge of guilt?

[ODYSSEUS]

This is different. Pyrrhus may be the son of Achilles, but he's just a boy.

[AGAMEMNON]

And what do you care? This isn't your son.

[AJAX]

Isn't he twelve?

[AGAMEMNON]

And already as quick as his father.

[AJAX]
Eleven?

[AGAMEMNON]
He's the next Aristos Achaion.

[AJAX / ODYSSEUS]
Ten? / I sure hope not.

[AJAX]
Of course you wouldn't want him to / be the next—

[ODYSSEUS]
/ Aristos Achaion means nothing and we all know it.

[AJAX] *suddenly enraged*
Then what, Odysseus? If that's what you really think, then
what are you doing here? Why are you sleeping on rocks and
feasting on bones? What is it exactly that you've given up ten
precious years of your life for? Was this all for nothing?

Phoenix shifts, and everyone looks over at him.

[ODYSSEUS] *subdued*
The loss of Achilles and Patroclus nearly killed him, sir. Don't
let him lose another son.

[AGAMEMNON]
Does he look like he's got many years left in him?

[ODYSSEUS]

Sir.

[AGAMEMNON]

End this nightmare. Let him die at home.

[AJAX]

May we all have the pleasure.

[AGAMEMNON]

This boy will win the war for us, Odysseus. Finish what
you've started.

[ODYSSEUS]

And how many more children do we have to sacrifice to win
this war?

*Agamemnon stares at Odysseus for a moment, then stands up and
leaves without a word. Phoenix, too, is watching quietly, having been
awake this whole time.*

[AJAX]

I'm not drunk enough for this.

*Ajax rises with a haunted look and also begins to leave. He goes back
to adjust Phoenix's blanket—and seeing Phoenix awake, is unsure what
to do with himself, eventually turning away again and exiting.
Odysseus and Phoenix are alone. Phoenix gazes at Odysseus.*

[PHOENIX]

Did I ever tell you about the oak tree on

the hill behind the running path?

Odysseus rises and goes to Phoenix.

[ODYSSEUS]
Yes, Phoenix. You told us not too long ago.

He adjusts Phoenix's blankets, and the two settle into silence.

XXII

PYRRHUS

*E*arly morning in the camp. Talthybius is bringing Briseis to Odysseus' tent. Her arms are full of laundry. The herald retreats, and Odysseus speaks to her quietly.

[ODYSSEUS]
I have arranged it. I'm sailing to Skyros at noon, and you will come with me. If you have anything of value, pack it now.

[BRISEIS]
Just me?

A moment. Then, resignation.

[ODYSSEUS]
All three of you girls.

[BRISEIS]
Yes, sir.

[ODYSSEUS]

Be discreet. Go about your duties as if nothing is amiss. Show no sign that you are leaving for good.

[BRISEIS]

Yes, sir.

[ODYSSEUS]

You are coming onboard to serve the men. At least, so I will say. When I return for the funeral, I'll tell Agamemnon that the king's men took a fancy to you—you *three*—and he would only relinquish Pyrrhus if I offered you up.

[BRISEIS]

Yes, sir.

[ODYSSEUS]

Agamemnon wishes for you to become his again to allay his humiliation. If he knows that you will not be returning, he will put a swift end to our plan.

[BRISEIS]

Not to worry, sir. I know how to treat with Agamemnon.

[ODYSSEUS]

We've all had to learn. Run along. Tell your friends the news.

Briseis leaves Odysseus' tent with her laundry. A secret smile on her face, she picks up her pace, nearly running.

Enter Pyrrhus, a bow and a quiver of arrows strapped to his back. He is twelve years old and does his best to carry himself like a warrior—a charade that is severely undermined by the fact that he is soaking wet. Briseis bumps into him and drops some of her laundry.

[BRISEIS]

I am so sorry, sir.

He reaches down to pick up the fallen garments.

[PYRRHUS]

That's all right. I'm sorry for being in your way. I'm looking for King Agamemnon. Do you know where his tent is?

[BRISEIS]

Yes, sir. I can take you. Is it your first time in the camp, sir?

[PYRRHUS]

We arrived this morning from Skyros. I have gathered what men I could and sailed here to offer our service.

[BRISEIS]

From Skyros?

[PYRRHUS]

Oh—I am Prince Pyrrhus, son of Achilles.

[BRISEIS]

Prince Pyrrhus.

[PYRRHUS]

I'm sorry. I never got your name.

She is surprised by the question.

[BRISEIS]

I am Princess Briseis of Lyrnessus.

[PYRRHUS]

Briseis?

I've heard a lot about you.

[BRISEIS]

Yes, sir,

[PYRRHUS]

So you knew my father well?

[BRISEIS]

I'd say so, sir. Better than most.

[PYRRHUS]

Of course, I've heard the stories about him. We all have. But there are many things I have wondered. Maybe you'd know. You will tell me everything sometime?

[BRISEIS]

Yes, sir. Actually—let me take you to Odysseus. He will be a better guide than I. He can help you around and bring you to Agamemnon.

[PYRRHUS]

Prince Odysseus?

[BRISEIS]

Yes, sir.

[PYRRHUS]

The man who brought my father to Troy?

Briseis is apprehensive, carefully watching his reaction.

[BRISEIS]

I think that is the one.

She had nothing to fear: Pyrrhus is dazzled by his own enthusiasm. Briseis begins to lead him to Odysseus' tent.

[PYRRHUS]

I've heard much of Odysseus, too. *Prince* Odysseus. He's become something of a legend on Skyros. For the short time he was there, he made quite an impression. I don't know if it's true or not, but they say he—

They have arrived at their destination. Odysseus is staring at Pyrrhus.

[BRISEIS]

This young man was looking for Agamemnon, sir.

[PYRRHUS]

Good morning, sir.

[ODYSSEUS]
What's your name, my boy?

[PYRRHUS]
Pyrrhus of Skyros, son of Achilles, sir.

[ODYSSEUS]
How did you come here?

[PYRRHUS]
By boat, sir.

[ODYSSEUS]
Yes, I presumed. I meant—

[PYRRHUS]
Oh. I heard news that my father was fallen, so I sailed here to offer up my service. Or has the war already been won?

[ODYSSEUS] *numbly*
Not quite. We are pleased to have you.

[PYRRHUS]
I have heard stories about you since I was small.

[ODYSSEUS]
I am afraid to hear of my reputation on Skyros. I will take you to Agamemnon. I imagine he will be delighted to see you.

[PYRRHUS]
I'm glad to hear that.

[ODYSSEUS]

Briseis, thank you for bringing the young man to me.

[BRISEIS]

Yes, sir.

[PYRRHUS]

If it is all right with you, sir, I would like her to come with us.
I wanted to talk further with her about my father.

[ODYSSEUS]

I don't see why not. Come along, Briseis.

Briseis silently joins them.

XXIII

BRISEIS' FLIGHT

P *yrrhus fidgets with the strap of his quiver as he, Briseis, and Odysseus all stand before the comfortably seated Agamemnon. Talthybius is posted outside Agamemnon's tent.*

[AGAMEMNON]

You waited so long, Odysseus, that the boy came himself.
Prince Pyrrhus, son of Achilles, as I live and breathe?

[PYRRHUS]

My father's son.

[AGAMEMNON]

Well, I'll be damned. Where are all your men?

[PYRRHUS]

They're docking the boats by now, sir. I swam ahead to let you
know they were coming.

[AGAMEMNON]

Don't you have guards or messengers or anything?

[PYRRHUS]

I was eager to meet you, sir.

[AGAMEMNON]

Well, we're sure glad to see you. Tell your men they can pitch their tents down the beach. Your father's tent should still be there. If the wind hasn't knocked it down by now, it's all yours. Odysseus, show him where.

[ODYSSEUS]

Can a herald be sent, sir? I promised Phoenix I would come fix his lunch right about now.

[AGAMEMNON]

He'll want to see the boy, won't he? Bring him along, then.

A beat.

[ODYSSEUS]

Come along, Pyrrhus. We don't want to keep Phoenix waiting.

[PYRRHUS]

Yes, sir. Honored to have met you, King Agamemnon. So long, Briseis.

Agamemnon acknowledges him with a brusque nod, Briseis with respectfully averted eyes.

Odysseus allows Pyrrhus to go ahead of him. As he walks out, he lets the cloak slip from his shoulders. It lies in Agamemnon's eyeline. He and Pyrrhus exit.

[AGAMEMNON]

Just like his father.

[BRISEIS]

How do you mean, sir?

[AGAMEMNON]

You would know. You were his.

[BRISEIS]

I was very lucky, sir.

[AGAMEMNON]

You were indeed. But now, his son has come to take his place.
And everything else that was his.

[BRISEIS]

Yes, sir.

[AGAMEMNON]

I almost think the kid deserves to have you. His father would
be alive if not for you.

[BRISEIS]

I never meant any harm, sir.

[AGAMEMNON]

In fact, a lot of good men would still be alive.

[BRISEIS]

That was not my doing, sir.

[AGAMEMNON] *dangerous*
Oh? Tell me. Whose was it, Briseis?

[BRISEIS]
Sir, if you won't be needing anything from me, I should go
along and make ready the meal.

[AGAMEMNON]
You leave when I say you can leave. Do you understand?

[BRISEIS]
MY GOOD LORD, MY APOLOGIES FOR CROSSING YOU
YOU CAN NAME ANY CONSEQUENCE—
I WILL BOW TO YOU
BUT YOU KNOW THAT I CAUSED NOTHING

[AGAMEMNON]
QUIT THIS STALLING, QUIT THIS BLUSHING

[BRISEIS]
YES, MY LORD

Agamemnon advances on her. Briseis moves in the other direction,
leading the commander with her.

MY GOOD LORD, IS THERE SOMETHING THAT YOU
WANT FROM ME?

[AGAMEMNON]
YOU DISGRACE ME TO MY MEN AND NOW YOU'RE
TAUNTING ME?

She is now backed against the table with nowhere to escape. She is exactly where she wants to be.

[BRISEIS]
WHILE I CANNOT CHANGE THE PAST, I
SWEAR TO ZEUS THAT IT'S THE LAST TIME
I'LL OFFEND

Briseis stabs Agamemnon with her dagger. Taking advantage of his momentary distraction, she runs out of the tent. By the time Agamemnon has picked up the weapon and realized that it is barely more than a toy, Briseis is gone.

Agamemnon stumbles after her. Odysseus, who follows Pyrrhus into the tent, attempts to sit the man down to check for wounds. Agamemnon pushes Odysseus away and goes in pursuit, Talthybius following him.

Briseis runs through the shallow water out to the sheer ocean cliffs—the cliffs that no Greek can climb—and begins to scale them. Iphis and Diomede enter—and seeing what is happening, drop their baskets of laundry and hurry to the shore to watch. A crowd of soldiers and captives alike gathers at the bottom of the cliffs, watching her ascent.

[IPHIS]
I WAS NEVER KNOWN FOR MY REVERENCE

[AGAMEMNON] *to Ajax*
Pursue her.

[IPHIS]
BUT I PRAY THAT OUR GODS ARE GENEROUS

[AJAX]
We can't, sir.

[DIOMEDE]
'CAUSE IT'S ALMOST LIKE SHE'S CHANGING

[IPHIS & DIOMEDE]
LIKE THE WIND BECOMES HER WINGS AND
HOW SHE FLIES

*The chorus of captives watches Briseis' flight, vocalizing behind Iphis
and Diomede. Pyrrhus rushes to watch.*

THEN THE FARAWAY MAN CALLS, / "BRISEIS"

[AGAMEMNON]
/ Briseis!

[IPHIS & DIOMEDE]
WHERE WE STAND, WE CAN SEE THE
SHORES OF TENEDOS
HOPE IS RISING UP TO MEET HER
SHE IS FLYING TOWARDS HER FREEDOM
TOWARDS THE SKY

*Briseis pulls herself onto the top of the cliff. She breaks into a run.
Thetis, too, comes to watch, standing apart from the rest.*

[DIOMEDE]
AND THERE'S NONE WHO COULD HAVE TOUCHED
HER THEN. NOT ONE.

In a sudden motion, Pyrrhus takes up his bow and notches his arrow.
He lets it go just as Briseis leaps into the air.

[IPHIS]
BUT A BOY WHO HAD TO BE HIS FATHER'S SON

Briseis dives. The arrow flies. Thetis steps forward. What happens
next is unclear. All that is apparent is that we do not see Briseis hit the
water, nor do we see the arrow pierce her, though everything happens so
quickly that no one can quite be sure of what they just witnessed. Briseis
is gone—that is all that matters to Agamemnon.

Agamemnon claps Pyrrhus on the back, congratulating him.
Odysseus is still. The captives huddle in grief, shock, wonder, and hope,
murmurously debating what they saw. Thetis watches, steadfast.

[PYRRHUS]
AND I PRAY THAT HER GODS ARE GENEROUS

Agamemnon and Pyrrhus exit. Though Agamemnon motions for
Odysseus to come, the man does not budge. The captives exit slowly,
glancing back several times as they go. Finally, Odysseus, too, turns
away and exits.

Iphis and Diomede are the last to leave—besides Thetis. As they pass
the woman, they both pause a moment to look at her, apparently the
only ones to notice her. She acknowledges them. With quiet hope, Iphis

and Diomede begin to leave. Thetis raises her arms, creating a familiar shadow puppet. Behind them, the shadow of a bird rises into the air.

Thetis watches the bird fly. Then, she exits.

Iphis turns back. She points out the bird to Diomede. Diomede makes the same shape with her hands, and they exit laughing.

Music. The days pass; the lights and shadows change. The war ends, and the Greeks enter one last time to disassemble the tents and clear the beach.

Odysseus is the last to leave. At last, he sets off for home.

XXIV

MEMORY

*T*he stage is dark and empty with a single shaft of light from up high. Odysseus enters in travel-worn attire, carrying a box.

[ODYSSEUS]
That's it. I can't say I remember the rest.

I can't say I've forgotten, either. I would be lying if I said I did.

Patroclus enters. His attire markedly contrasts with Odysseus', designating him as one of the dead.

[PATROCLUS]
I didn't think you had any qualms about that.

[ODYSSEUS]
About what?

[PATROCLUS]
Twisting your words here and there. Dressing the truth in borrowed armor.

[ODYSSEUS]

I do consider that one of my finest talents.

[PATROCLUS]

I would think so, considering…

Odysseus catches his meaning, but does not respond.

You never told anyone?

[ODYSSEUS]

I'll take it to the grave.

[PATROCLUS]

It looks like you have. I'm sorry to see you here.

[ODYSSEUS]

Don't be. I'm not—at least I don't think I am—

[PATROCLUS]

You're not, are you?

[ODYSSEUS]

I was on my way home after the war was won. There have
been complications. I was told to travel here for guidance to find
my way back to my wife and son.

[PATROCLUS]

You haven't received it?

[ODYSSEUS]

I've seen far too many familiar faces. It was you I sought out.

[PATROCLUS]

Why?

[ODYSSEUS]

I was hoping to receive your blessing.

[PATROCLUS]

Mine?

[ODYSSEUS]

Forgive me, Patroclus.

[PATROCLUS]

It's more than just my life that you threw over.

[ODYSSEUS]

Tell me what I must do to appease your soul.

[PATROCLUS]

You know it's too late for that.

[ODYSSEUS]

Patroclus. Believe me when I say that I understand what it is

to—

[PATROCLUS]

To gaze at him sleeping, falling into the spaces between the
breaths, wondering if this is how he'll look in death? To hold him

through his grief, to feel his hot tears and to be glad, desperately glad, because it reminds you that he is alive? You never understood, Odysseus.

[ODYSSEUS]
Then tell me.

[PATROCLUS]
I LOOK TOWARDS
THE DISTANCE
HE'S CALLING MY NAME

I'M RUNNING
TO MEET HIM
HE GRINS AND HE WAITS

I WISH I HAD A SECRET
I WISH I HAD A THOUSAND
AND JUST SO I COULD TELL HIM EVERY SINGLE ONE

AND THEN I START TO SEE IT
I DON'T KNOW HOW TO SAY IT
IT'S SOMETHING LIKE A QUESTION BUT IT ALWAYS
COMES UNDONE

IF HE HAD NOT BEEN MINE
IF HE HAD NOT BEEN MINE...

Thetis enters from the darkness. Gone is her shimmering divine cast. She is dressed in grey: mortal, real.

[THETIS]
I'M STANDING ALONE AND
THE WIND STEALS MY BREATH

I FEEL THE STORM APPROACHING
YOU KNOW WHAT COMES NEXT

THEN SOMETHING BURNS INSIDE ME
IT'S SOMETHING LIKE A SECRET
AT TIMES, IT FEELS LIKE ANGER; AT TIMES, LIKE
PRIDE

I HOLD HIM LIKE A GRUDGE AND YET
I KEEP HIM LIKE A PROMISE
I KNOW I DIDN'T CHOOSE HIM BUT I KNOW THAT HE
IS MINE

IF HE HAD NOT BEEN MINE
IF HE HAD NOT BEEN MINE...

Dressed as they were in the first scene, Young Patroclus runs onstage with a lyre as Young Achilles tries to take it back from him. The three watch.

One by one, the ensemble of shades enters behind them, humming quiet harmonies under the dialogue.

[PATROCLUS]
Achilles, racing down the hill, laughing and reaching for my hand. / Achilles

[THETIS]

/ Achilles, the son I never wanted to bear. / Achilles

Middle Achilles and Middle Patroclus enter, dueling across the stage
with wooden swords.

[PATROCLUS]

/ Achilles, gazing at the sea, his eyes bright with longing. His
voice brave and breaking. To Troy, / he says—

Phoenix enters, clothed in gray, standing with Thetis, watching the
boys as they play.

[PHOENIX]

/ he says to me that he will not rise to fight. And when he says
those words, I see the way their looks darken, / the way—

[PATROCLUS]

/ the way the light teased joy from his eyes. His fingers running through his hair. His face honest with morning sunlight. /
His

[THETIS]

/ His father's gentle, bruising hands. The waves that once sang
"home," now whispering of the day that man came to the sea and
took me. The water turning grey as the morning dies, / as—

Dressed as the other shades are, Priam enters, stepping forth from
the crowd to stand in constellation with Thetis and Phoenix.

[PRIAM]

/ as dawn spills blood over Troy. As he arms for battle one last time, shouldering his armor and that quiet sadness. Something lonely in his stride. / Something—

[ODYSSEUS]

/ Something crumbling as I hold my son for the last time. / Something

[THETIS]

/ Something tearing, breaking. / Something—

[PATROCLUS]

/ Something bending, yielding. / Something—

[THETIS]

/ Something aching, rising, swelling like the tide. My child growing inside me:

[THETIS & PRIAM]

my vengeance

[THETIS, PHOENIX, & PRIAM]

and my hope.

[PATROCLUS]

Everything,

[THETIS]

I vowed.

[THETIS, PHOENIX, & PRIAM]
Everything they took from me.

[PATROCLUS, THETIS, PHOENIX, ODYSSEUS, PRIAM]
I will give this boy everything.

Middle Achilles and Middle Patroclus run out. Young Achilles lingers behind with his lyre, which he has finally wrestled back into his possession. Young Patroclus tries to tug at him to come along. Finally, Young Patroclus exits without him, looking back all the while. Young Achilles retreats into the shadows.

[PATROCLUS]
TOO EARLY TO TELL HIM
TOO LATE TO FORGET
I'M COUNTING DOWN FROM TWENTY
AND TIME HOLDS ITS BREATH

[PATROCLUS, THETIS, PHOENIX]
THE MEMORIES COME LIKE RAINFALL
THE EARTH IS CRUSHED TO SWEETNESS
AND EVERYTHING IS HOLY AND TURNS TO GOLD

[THETIS]
HIS HAIR ABOUT HIS SHOULDERS

[PATROCLUS]
IT TANGLES WITH THE SUNLIGHT

[PATROCLUS, THETIS, PRIAM, & PHOENIX]
AND SOMEHOW I ALREADY KNOW I WON'T SEE HIM
GROW OLD

IF HE HAD NOT BEEN MINE
IF HE HAD NOT BEEN MINE
IF HE HAD NOT BEEN MINE
THEN WHAT WOULD I HAVE BEEN?

[ODYSSEUS / PATROCLUS]
HE SWORE THAT HE WOULD GO WITH YOU / HE
TURNED FROM TOMORROW
HE SAID HE'D BE THERE TOMORROW / AND YOU ARE
THE REASON
AND THOUGH YOU CAME TO TROY / AND YOU ARE
THE REASON
HE SOMEHOW STAYED THAT BOY
AND YOU ARE THE REASON

All the shades disperse and exit, leaving only Patroclus and Odysseus,
with Young Achilles in the shadows.

[PATROCLUS]
Tell me about your son.

[ODYSSEUS]
I can't.

[PATROCLUS]
I understand.

[ODYSSEUS]

No. I mean that—I was called to sail to Skyros just after he was born. I was taken from him when he was days old. I never knew him.

I would imagine raising him. I would spin all manner of anecdotes from his boyhood, and I would tell them to anyone in the camp who would listen, and I would almost believe them. I see a different boy in my head every night, almost like I have a thousand sons. Sometimes he looks like you.

[PATROCLUS]

He does?

[ODYSSEUS]

Sometimes he looks like Achilles.

There is one memory I do have with him. A lullaby I sang to him every night, even before we brought him into the world. An old song. A springtime song.

Patroclus wonders if it could be the same lullaby.

[ODYSSEUS & PATROCLUS]
TOMORROW PERHAPS—

Like a change in the wind, like a sudden shift of light, Young Achilles appears with his lyre. He is the boy Patroclus once knew. He is the son Odysseus never knew. Patroclus and Odysseus gaze at him with sorrow and wonder.

[YOUNG ACHILLES]
Not again.

[PATROCLUS]
I'm not finished.

TOMORROW PERHAPS—

[YOUNG ACHILLES]
Chiron is waiting for us.

[PATROCLUS] *to Odysseus*
Achilles told me—

[YOUNG ACHILLES]
TOMORROW PERHAPS I WILL
SLEEP PAST THE SUNRISE
AND FIND THAT YOU'D GONE IN THE NIGHT

[PATROCLUS]
TIE WINGS TO MY SANDALS, I'LL DRINK FROM THE
SKY

[YOUNG ACHILLES, PATROCLUS, & ODYSSEUS]
AND I'LL BE BY YOUR SIDE BY AND BY

'CAUSE WHERE YOU GO

[YOUNG ACHILLES]
I WILL GO WITH

[YOUNG ACHILLES & PATROCLUS / ODYSSEUS]
I WILL GO WITH YOU / I CANNOT FOLLOW
OH, DON'T YOU KNOW / OH, DON'T YOU KNOW
MY CHILDHOOD IS IN YOUR EYES / TOMORROW WAS
IN YOUR EYES

Young Achilles is retreating once again, and the orchestration dwindles down to one or two instruments.

[PATROCLUS / ODYSSEUS]
I WILL GO WITH YOU / I CANNOT FOLLOW
I WILL GO WITH YOU / I CANNOT FOLLOW
I WILL GO WITH YOU— / I CANNOT FOLLOW—

The melody hangs unresolved. Young Achilles exits. Patroclus looks at the box Odysseus is carrying.

[PATROCLUS]
You shouldn't stay amongst us too long. Leave your offering and go.

[ODYSSEUS]
This isn't an offering. I brought a handful of your ashes with me. Yours and Achilles'. I wanted to bring them back to Mount Pelion.

[PATROCLUS]
You've lingered with us long enough. Scatter them to the winds. You find your way and we'll find ours. Go home, Odysseus.

[ODYSSEUS]

You didn't get to.

[PATROCLUS]

But you do. So tell our story.

[ODYSSEUS]

What good will it do you?

[PATROCLUS]

I don't know. Perhaps it will do you some.

[ODYSSEUS]

What shall I say?

[PATROCLUS]

Say that there were two boys who raced each other to the sunrise. Say that one went too far, and the other went with him.

[ODYSSEUS]

And how should I end it?

[PATROCLUS]

However you'd like. Turn us into trees. Or change us into birds. Hang us in the stars, if your gods are generous.

[ODYSSEUS]

What would you become?

[PATROCLUS]

What?

[ODYSSEUS]
If the gods could change you, what would you become?

[PATROCLUS]
Anything.

[ODYSSEUS]
Anything?

[PATROCLUS]
Anything. I'd become whatever he does.

[ODYSSEUS]
You did.

A boy. A man.

[PATROCLUS]
A lover.

[ODYSSEUS]
A fool.

[PATROCLUS]
A soldier.

[ODYSSEUS]
A hero.

Best of the Myrmidons.

Patroclus is retreating.

Best of the Greeks.

Aristos Achaion.

Patroclus has gone, and Odysseus is standing alone. He turns to go, walking back towards the light. Then, he pauses, turns around, and reaches into his box. Over the Memory theme, he tosses the ashes and they catch the wind, turning to gold in the brightening sunlight.

The Memory Theme falls gently and the lights warm to drowsy summer. Followed by silhouetted Chiron—now the great centaur of myth—Young Achilles and Young Patroclus enter, chasing each other across the stage, spectral and unreal in the rapidly brightening light.

Odysseus watches them go, and then turns to leave himself. The golden light engulfs the entire stage and then snaps to blackout.

Curtain.

END OF SHOW

WHO IS THIS BOY?

Muse Lee is a Korean-Chinese artist based in Los Angeles.

Muse's writing, theatre, and mythology pursuits collided when he (accidentally) invited a bunch of kids to perform some songs he'd written, thus creating *Aristos:* the Musical, a queer *Iliad* adaptation that has gone global despite his best efforts to go to grad school. For his work with *Aristos*, Muse was appointed a 2021-22 Harvard University Center for Hellenic Studies Visiting Artist.

Beyond *Aristos*, he is a Trekkie, an opera nerd, a burgeoning dad rock enthusiast, and a somewhat begrudging recipient of a BA in English from Stanford University. He cherishes his experiences teaching the arts in schools, prison, and juvenile hall, as well as his wealth of concerning stories from his many weird jobs. He is proudly transmasculine and aroace.

He apologizes for the bathroom selfie, but headshots are expensive and he quite likes the jacket.

"You are the dreamer and the dream."

Instagram: @biasinboy